I0236680

BREWERIES AND MALTINGS:

THEIR

ARRANGEMENT, CONSTRUCTION, MACHINERY, AND PLANT.

By GEORGE SCAMELL, F.R.I.B.A., F.G.S.

SECOND EDITION,

Revised, Enlarged, and partly Re-written,

By FREDERICK COLYER, M. Inst. C.E., M.I.M.E.,
BREWERS' CONSULTING ENGINEER AND ARCHITECT.

LONDON:
E. & F. N. SPON, 46, CHARING CROSS.
NEW YORK:
446, BROOME STREET.
1880.

The *Patent List* has been revised and brought up to the present time; the accuracy of this may be relied upon.

Nearly all the drawings in this edition are new, and are prepared from works that have been executed in various parts of the kingdom.

It is hoped the work in its present form will be as favourably received as the first edition; no effort has been spared to render it equally acceptable.

All "brewing" questions have, as before, been omitted, the architectural and engineering features being only treated.

Since going to press, alterations have been proposed in the Excise duties which will modify to some extent the construction of malt houses, especially as far as the old restrictions are concerned.

As regards the brewery department, it being proposed to take the duty at the fermenting tuns, some alterations in the plant may be required to carry out the new system, but nothing definite has yet been settled.

FREDERICK COLYER, M. Inst. C.E., M.I.M.E.,
Brewers' Consulting Engineer and Architect.

18, GREAT GEORGE STREET, WESTMINSTER, S.W.,
June, 1880.

PREFACE TO SECOND EDITION.

The first edition of this work having been so well received, and as it has now been out of print some time, from the numerous inquiries that have been made it was determined to issue a second edition, and to enlarge and nearly re-write the whole matter, adding all the latest improvements in plant and construction up to the present time.

In undertaking the above, I have endeavoured to make the book acceptable not only to brewers, but to anyone requiring practical information as to the construction of this class of work.

I have carefully avoided mentioning any special kind of manufacture, following the original idea of the first edition; at the same time, I believe all plant, machinery, and apparatus used either in a large or small brewery, &c., has been described in detail. The book being designed for practical men, a short, terse description is only given.

Chapters I., III., IV., VIII., IX., XIII., XVII., XVIII., &c., have been entirely re-written, and all the other chapters have been revised, and much new matter added.

been prepared from work upon which the author has been engaged in different parts of the kingdom.

The plans and sections given have been specially prepared for this work by the author, and have been designed with a view to secure economy as well as efficiency in working.

To render the work more complete, a few tables and memoranda have been given, some of which have been calculated expressly for its pages, and will be found useful for the gauging of vessels, &c.

The List of Patents has been carefully arranged, specially for this work, and the author would advise anyone to refer to it before taking out a patent in connection with the subjects to which it refers.

The author takes this opportunity of acknowledging his obligations to many of his friends for the valuable suggestions and assistance rendered during his professional connection with them in past years.

GEORGE SCAMELL, F.R.I.B.A., F.G.S.

18, GREAT GEORGE STREET, WESTMINSTER, S.W.

PREFACE TO FIRST EDITION.

The author, during his practical experience in the various departments connected with the erection of breweries and maltings, with their relative machinery and plant, acquired during an engagement extending over a period of some years in the engineering department of Messrs. Truman, Hanbury, Buxton, & Co.'s brewery, and subsequently as brewers' consulting engineer and architect, has frequently heard the desire expressed by persons interested in the erection and working of breweries for some treatise upon the various important points involved in their arrangement and construction. The following pages have been prepared to meet this desideratum. The information has been given in a general form, as without knowing the special circumstances under which the various appliances require to be arranged and the machines to work, it might only have misled had any particular arrangement or make been mentioned and recommended. But the author will always be happy to afford any further information upon receiving particulars of the circumstance under which the machinery will have to work.

The estimates given as to the cost of erecting have

CONTENTS.

BREWERIES AND MALTINGS.

CHAPTER I.

SITE—GENERAL PRINCIPLE FOR ARRANGEMENT OF BUILDINGS.

In selecting a site for the erection of a brewery, several matters have to be taken into consideration, the first and most important being the water supply, both as to quantity and quality. If any doubt exists respecting this, it will be advisable to sink a trial bore-hole; should the result prove unsatisfactory, the sum spent in boring will have been well expended, having prevented a larger outlay, which would have proved, if not altogether a dead loss, yet nearly unremunerative. Many breweries have, however, been erected, and are now being worked satisfactorily in towns brewing from water supplied by the water companies, using the well water, which may not be suitable for brewing purposes, for refrigerating and washing. In some few instances the water supplied by the companies is used for all purposes, ice-making machinery being employed in the summer months for refrigerating.

When the water supply is decided, the next consideration is the position with regard to other buildings, as it is very advantageous to place a brewery in an open and airy site, particular care being taken to avoid the immediate vicinity of any gas-works or other factories from which offensive odours are given off. This is a most important consideration, as, according to our best authorities, such odours prove detrimental to the production of a good, sound, and well-flavoured article. The disposal of the drainage also requires consideration; if a brewery is situated some distance from a town, it may be necessary to erect settling and filtering tanks, because, should the sewage be allowed to pass direct into a stream or ditch in the summer months, it is certain to create a nuisance. As a rule, a perfectly level site is *not* to be preferred, as might naturally be supposed, to a site on rising ground, as the slope can generally be taken advantage of by placing the section of the building which contains the various utensils so that one will command another, saving pumping and labour, without necessitating any part of the buildings being a great height. Another point to be considered with regard to the site is the means of conveying the raw materials to the brewery, and delivering the beer. Arrangements should be made, where possible, to have a railway siding alongside, or the brewery may be placed with advantage on the banks of a river or canal, whereby the expense of cartage may be saved.

In selecting a site, particular attention should be

paid to the nature of the soil with a view to securing a good and sound foundation. This is essential, seeing the great weight which the foundations have to carry. Trial holes should be opened, especially at points where treacherous soils are expected. Wherever any doubt exists as to the soundness of the soil, a layer of concrete should be placed in the bottom of the foundation trench on which the footings of the superincumbent wall rest. In the use of concrete, care should be taken to make it of good quality, to lay it properly in the trench, and to see that the layer be of sufficient thickness.

When concrete is to be used, it should be done under competent advice, as well for securing it of good quality as for the laying it down in a proper way. Soils viewed as foundation soils may be divided into three classes, on the peculiar features of each of which a few words may here be usefully given. To the first class belong solid rock, compact stony soil, some tufas and hard clay which yield only to the pick. These are practically incompressible, or if compressible, only in a degree so slight as not to affect the stability of the heaviest mass of masonry or brickwork which may be laid upon them, as they do not yield in a lateral direction. In some foundation soils of this class, fissures of greater or less width are sometimes met with which require certain precautions in forming the bottom. Slaty or shaly rocks require the greatest care in preparing for the foundations, as although when opened up they at first present a perfectly hard substance, they are apt to disintegrate or yield under the influence of the atmosphere and rain. In such cases the foundations should be formed as rapidly as possible after the soil is opened up, and concrete may require to be judiciously used. In soils of this description, in stony earth and hard clays, the foundation trenches should be made of such depths as will enable the compact soil to be reached beneath the zone influenced by hard frosts, which have a tendency to loosen or disintegrate the soil. To the second class of foundation soils belong gravel and sand. These are practically incompressible under a heavy weight, but require in some cases to be confined at the sides to prevent them spreading out laterally; should they have this tendency to give way, special means must be taken to prevent it. In sand, water is often met with, in which case special precautions will have to be taken.

Although we have put these soils under two classes in the order of their value, a soil of the second class may, nevertheless, be really a first-class soil. Thus gravel may be, and often is, found in such a condition that it may be ranked as a first-class soil for foundations, while clay may, on the other hand, be anything but a first-class soil. Indeed, in some cases there is no description of soil so treacherous and uncertain as this.

These remarks point to the importance of the strictest attention being paid to the filling in of good foundation trenches. To the third class of soils belong all the varieties which have a tendency to move laterally; such soils require peculiar care, and the methods by which a good foundation is secured vary with circumstances. When clay puddling is used, the most scrupulous attention should be given to the placing of the layers of puddle. The thinner these layers are, the more compact will be the puddle when well rammed; it is a great mistake to use too thick layers.

Designing a Brewery.

In planning a brewery, there are a few general principles to be considered, which we will now briefly point out. In the first place, the various utensils should be so designed as to allow the extension of the plant at a future time without disturbing the general arrangement. As far as possible the brewery should be designed to work by gravitation, avoiding all pumping (except pumping the liquor into the tank); that is, the hot liquor back should command the mash tun, the mash tun the underback and copper, the copper the hop back, and from the hop back the wort should flow to the coolers or receiver, and through the refrigerator to the fermenting tuns, &c. This arrangement, however good and economical, can seldom be carried out in practice in large breweries, it being obvious that part at least of the buildings must be carried to a great height. The more usual plan is to arrange the plant in such a way that the liquor gravitates to the hop back, the wort is then pumped to the coolers; it is considered by most brewers better to pump the "boiled" than the "raw wort." Again, by this arrangement there is a considerable saving of expense in erecting the coppers; if erected at a level sufficiently high to command the coolers, it necessitates carrying up heavy brickwork or ironwork to support them, and there is the constant expense of hoisting coal for working, entailing an amount of extra labour. As a general principle it is desirable to have the boilers, coppers, and hop back in a distinct building, as it keeps the brewery free from steam. The boilers should be so placed as to allow of their being removed when worn out without cutting them to pieces, so that new boilers can be taken in whole, as the work is not so sound if a boiler has to be riveted up after delivery. For small plants, when boiling by steam and where space is confined, it is occasionally advantageous to pump the "raw wort" and place the copper at the top of the building. The mash tun and hop back should be so situated that the grains and spent hops may be easily got rid of.

The tun-room windows should face the north, and if of large size the walls should be built hollow, so that the temperature of the room may remain at an equal degree all the year round. The roofs of tun room and over cooler should be tiled, as they resist heat better than slates, and in the case of the cooler the vapour from the wort is absorbed by the tiles, and is not condensed to drop back into the wort; where slates are used over tun rooms the ceilings should be *plastered*.

The malt and hop lofts should be kept as close and as air-tight as possible; but in all other parts there should be thorough ventilation. It is generally considered that malt keeps best in deep bins. These should be lined throughout with boards; if the malt comes in contact with any external walls it is liable to become slack. These boards should be movable, in order to facilitate the removal of vermin; divisions between the bins, if made of iron plates, do not form a harbour for weevils. Separate rooms must be provided for roasted malt and sugar, according to the Excise regulations.

Drains.—In arranging these, the following points should be considered. They should be laid out in straight lines and in as true gradients as possible; there should be cesspools at intervals for cleaning out, as on account of the quantity of spent hops, grains, &c., which get washed down, especially from the cooperage, the drains in a brewery are very liable to get choked. All inlets should be properly protected and fitted with traps. If the rain-water pipes are connected to the drains they can act as ventilating pipes; in this case the joints must be made tight with lead. The best drains are constructed of earthenware pipes jointed with cement; where junctions occur they should not join at right angles, but should have easy bends. A good fall, not less than 1 inch in 10 feet, should be given.

Floors, as far as possible, should be constructed fireproof, either brick, or concrete arches carried on iron girders and covered with asphalte, the small additional expense above wood floors being more than balanced by the advantages gained in the ease with which the buildings may be kept sweet by flushing the floors with an abundance of cold water, asphalte being impervious to damp, &c.

For the floors of cellars, and for the ground floors, the best materials in use are concrete and asphalte. Stone flags, stone blocks, tiles, or bricks, however good in some respects, do not give surfaces which are so easily kept clean as those formed of either the above-named materials. One advantage presented by asphalte and concrete should alone decide the point in their favour against any other material, and that is that floors formed of them present a perfectly uniform surface, having no joints or cracks into which dirt or water can get or lodge. In the formation of asphalte floors the greatest care is required; unless this is exercised, "faults" will prevail in the form of cracks and hollow places worse than in the case of floors formed of stone, brick, or tiles. To ensure good work, a first-class foundation of concrete in Portland cement is absolutely necessary. This must be most carefully made, so as to have the whole surface uniform, hard, and unyielding throughout its whole extent. It is scarcely necessary to say that the asphalte used must be of first-rate quality. Some asphalte is so poor, very little better than coal-tar mixed with sand or other hard substance, that it is not deserving the name, and assuredly is not worthy of being used where good work is deemed, as it ought to be, essential. We have found the Seyssel Asphalte (Claridge's Patent) stand the heavy wear better than any other description.

But after considerable experience of its use, and having seen it applied under a wide variety of trying circumstances, we would strongly recommend Portland cement concrete to be used for the foundations of cellar and other floors where solid floors are admissible. This material, if the work be properly executed, makes a floor quite equal to the best stone: it forms a beautiful surface, easily kept clean, impervious to wet, and is, therefore, a good means of preventing damp rising from the ground, and by consequence water used in cleaning the brewery from soaking into it. Gutters can be made in it with the greatest ease while laying the concrete, by simply using long pieces of timber, the edge of which is half-rounded, so as to give the desired width and depth to the groove. The whole operation of concrete floor-making is so simple that we have employed mere labourers, under a good foreman, to lay large surfaces, although they had no previous experience. Doubtless, some care is requisite to ensure a flat surface, and to give the required fall to the gutters, but a very little experience will give the workmen confidence in laying this kind of floor, which is in every respect the best for all working-rooms. The following is a brief description of the mode of making concrete, and preparing the "bottoming" of stones for the concrete to rest upon, which should be large enough to pass through a 2-inch or 1½-inch ring. The best material to use for making the concrete is crushed or ground brick or small clinkers (not of coke); if these cannot be obtained, good sharp sand, sea or river, will do (we have used both with success). The broken brick, clinkers, or sand, are well mixed with Portland cement in the proportion of three parts of material to one of the cement, water being added to bring the whole to such a consistency as to be easily spread upon the floor. Not much should be mixed at a time, as it "sets" rapidly. The spreading should be begun at one end of the space, and gradually brought down to the other end, so that what is done be not trampled upon. Where parts must be passed over before the concrete is "set," plank boards should be laid down. In forty-eight hours the surface will be quite hard enough to be walked over without injury, and in a week it will be as hard as stone, and will present the appearance of a floor of that material, solid, without a crack or flaw throughout its whole extent. Raised "flags" or stepping-stones may also be formed outside the door of concrete. The concrete is made two inches in thickness, and is laid upon the rough surface of the "bottoming," which is formed of broken bricks, or road metal, of size sufficient to pass through a 2-inch or $1\frac{3}{4}$-inch ring. The depth of this bottoming is four inches, and the upper surface should be carefully levelled before beginning to lay the concrete on the top of it; the full depth of the floor is, therefore, six inches.

"**Portland cement**" is made by mixing definite proportions of chalk and carbonate of lime with the argillaceous deposit of certain rivers, the waters of which flow over clay and chalk. In this country the Medway, or rather the bays and creeks on the sides of it, afford the best material. The cohesive strength of the cement made from these materials is very great—four times as much as that of the best hydraulic lime. When mixed with broken bricks it forms a concrete which is stronger than Portland stone in the proportion of 2·28 to 1·48. In purchasing Portland cement it is well to specify the weight per bushel. A good quality is that which weighs 110 lb. and upwards; some authorities prefer a lighter cement, as 100 to 105 lb., but experimental evidence is in favour of the heavier cement.

Iron being so generally used in construction, the following tables may be useful for reference. The first gives the safe load in tons that a cast-iron hollow column is calculated to bear; thickness of metal 1 inch:—

Length in Feet.	Outside Diameter in Inches.				
	5	6	7	8	9
	tons	tons	tons	tons	tons
8	23	34	46	58	71
10	19	28	39	51	63
12	14	23	33	44	55
16	10	16	24	32	42
20	6	11	17	24	33

For general work rolled iron joists are the most convenient girders to use, and they can now be obtained 16 inches deep, and up to 30 feet in length. The next table gives the safe load in cwts., the weight being distributed equally over the whole length of the girder:—

Depth.	Width of Flanges.	Bearing in Feet.					
		10	12	14	16	18	20
in.	in.	cwts.	cwts.	cwts.	cwts.	cwts.	cwts.
5	3	60	50	40	38	31	..
7	$3\frac{1}{2}$	120	100	84	73	64	56
9	$3\frac{3}{4}$	184	153	130	113	97	84
10	$4\frac{1}{2}$	312	224	190	165	144	128
12	5	440	377	320	275	238	210
14	6	650	540	500	400	360	320

In certain cases where it is important that the ironwork should be perfectly rigid—such as the supports for slate vessels—cast iron is to be preferred for girders. The next table has been calculated, giving the safe load in tons, equally distributed over the girder:—

Depth of Girder.	Width, Bottom Flange.	Thickness of Metal.	Length of Bearing in Feet.				
			10	12	15	17½	20
in.	in.	in.	tons	tons	tons	tons	tons
10	6	1	7·0	5·8	4·5	..	..
	8	1	9·5	8·0	6·6	5·0	..
12	8	1¼	14·0	11·7	9·0	8·0	7·0
	10	1¼	17·5	14·5	11·7	10·0	8·7
15	10	1½	26·0	22·0	18·0	15·0	13·0
	12	1½	31·5	26·0	21·0	18·0	15·7

CHAPTER II.

WELLS AND WATER.

The position of the well being decided upon, the next consideration is the way in which it should be constructed. If the water obtained from the well is to be used for brewing, it is necessary to construct the wall to keep out all surface water, which, as a rule, is contaminated, and charged with organic matter. Generally, for wells of a moderate depth, and sunk through clay or similar strata, it is sufficient to have a lining or steining of brickwork, which, for wells of small diameter, may be 4½ inches thick, and larger sizes 9 inches thick. The upper part of the steining should be executed in cement, or in mortar made with hydraulic lime or Portland cement concrete; if ordinary lime be used, the water will soon wash it out. In the remaining portion of the work the bricks should be laid dry, with occasional rings in cement or concrete. The method formerly employed for putting in the steining was to commence with a wooden curb upon which the bricks were placed. The earth was then removed below the curb, so as to allow the steining to settle; additional brick-work was added, and the excavation continued, this process being carried on till, from the swelling of the ground, the steining would be so tightly held that it could no longer settle. A second curb was then arranged inside the first, and the same process commenced again, the second excavation being as much smaller than the first as the thickness of the steining. The method now usually adopted, however, is to excavate as far as practically safe, depending upon the strata pierced, and to execute the steining of that portion, commencing with a ring in cement; a second portion is then excavated below the first, of the same diameter; and the steining is carried up to the under side of the first portion. Where, however, a well is to be constructed of a great depth, or through a sandy soil, or where it is necessary to sink through strong sand springs, although it may not be altogether impossible to execute the work as above described, yet it would be attended with an enormous amount of trouble. Under such circumstances, the modern practice is to line the well with iron cylinders instead of brickwork. The cylinders are made either of wrought or cast iron, cast iron being most usual in practice. The lower edge of the bottom or lowest cylinder is cast with a comparatively sharp or knife edge. The cylinder is placed in position, and the earth is excavated beneath it, allowing the cylinder to sink. A second cylinder is then placed on the top of the first and bolted to it, and additional earth is excavated, allowing the two cylinders to sink still further. This process is continued until the required depth has been obtained; care must be taken that the cylinders sink vertically. It is generally advisable to ascertain, by means of a bore-hole, the nature of the strata through which the well is to be sunk, as in the event of a strong spring being met with, it is often sufficient to bore a 6-inch to 10-inch hole, lining the same with a copper pipe, perforated at the lower end, and thus save the expense of cast-iron cylinders; it is also an advantage to have a good firm bed for the cylinders to rest on. The operation of boring is very simple in theory. The boring tools consist of a great variety of chisels used for cutting through rock and other hard substances; augers used in clayey or similar soils, and also for clearing the bore-hole. The boring rods are usually made of wrought iron from 10 to 20 feet long and from 1 to 1½ inch square, with a screw at one end and a socket at the other to connect them together, the first or top rod having a link for suspending the rods from, and immediately below this link are one or more holes for inserting the levers by which the boring tool is worked. If the well is of small diameter, as there would not be space for bringing sufficient leverage to bear upon the tools, it is necessary to work the tools from the surface. Where, however, the well is of large diameter, the tools are worked from a stage erected down the well. The mode of operation is as follows:—The selected tool is screwed to the lower rod, and a sufficient number of rods are connected, according to the depth of sinking through clay. It is sufficient to give a rotary motion to the rods, by means of levers inserted in the top rod, as before mentioned. Where, however, the strata to be pierced is of a hard nature, a cutting chisel is attached to the rods, which are lifted a short distance by any convenient method, and allowed to drop, until, by this percussive action, a certain depth is obtained, after which the rods are withdrawn, and the fragments are removed by an auger. Where the borings are continued to a great depth, there is necessarily a great strain upon the rods, which, in consequence, occasionally give way. To meet these cases, there are certain tools constructed for the purpose of extracting broken rods. Where the spring of water met with in the boring is not strong, it is often desirable to enlarge the bottom of the well considerably to collect the water, and form a good reservoir for the pumps to draw from. An instance of this occurs at Messrs. Truman, Hanbury, & Co.'s, the well at that establishment being excavated some way into the chalk. At this level two tunnels are constructed about 7′ 0″ × 3′ 0″, running north and south for about 100 feet each way.

In place of lining the wells with bricks, Portland cement concrete is now being used with great success. The operation is very easily carried out in soils of ordinary tenacity and firmness; greater difficulty is of course met with in the case of loose soil or running sand. Where the well is of no great depth and the soil firm, so that an excavation can be made at once, a drum is constructed, the external diameter of which is equal to the internal diameter of the well, the excavation being made so much greater in diameter than the drum, as the thickness of the concrete and lining of the well is intended to be,—9 inches is a thickness which will do in ordinary soil; the space left between the internal diameter of the excavation and the external diameter of the drum is filled or packed in with concrete, the depth of which packing is of course equal to the depth of the drum, which may be 18 inches or 2 feet —the top of packing should be level with the top of drum. The drum is then raised and supported by uprights and braces, another packing of concrete is made, the drum is again raised, and so on till the whole depth of excavation is lined with concrete. The bottom of the excavation should be lined with a layer of concrete 9 inches thick, and the top may be arched over, leaving a manhole door in centre, and a hole for the pump barrel to pass down. If the soil is not very sound, a drum had better be sunk from the top, filling in the concrete, excavating below the drum, lowering this, and again filling in the concrete lining.

The concrete should be made with the best Portland cement, 105 lb. to 112 lb. the bushel, this being mixed with broken brick passed through a pair of rollers, and the whole mixed with water, in sufficient quantity to make the concrete easily worked and filled in. The proportion of Portland cement used should be one part to every five or six parts of broken brick; some use as high a proportion of broken brick as eight to one of Portland cement; we prefer the lower proportion as giving the soundest work for well lining. Some part of this concrete may be saved by packing the centre of the lining with small stones. These should not be of larger dimensions than 3 inches diameter or thereabouts, but stones sufficient to pass through a 2½-inch ring will be better. The stones should be carefully packed, with some distance apart, so that the concrete when put into the mould will run between, and embrace them; when the concrete "sets," a very firm lining will be obtained.

Diamond Rock Boring.—Bore-holes for Well purposes, where any great depth is required, especially in hard strata, are now made by this ingenious process. The diamond drill works by rotation without striking a blow; the action when going through rock is rather abrading than cutting, the effect being produced by the difference in the hardness of the diamond and the rock. The diamonds are not valuable gems, but "carbonates," and were first introduced for cutting other diamonds. They are black, and quite unlike the ordinary brilliant diamond; are found in Brazil, and are worth about 15*s.* to 20*s.* per carat.

These stones are firmly set in an annular steel ring, leaving only sufficient projection to allow the water and débris to pass. This steel ring is attached to steel tubes, and kept rotating at 150 revolutions in soft, and 250 revolutions per minute in hard strata. Water is supplied from the centre to keep the tool cool, and rises at the sides, conveying débris to the surface. The tool is pressed forward with a force equal to from 400 lb. to 800 lb. when the cutting is done from 2 inches to 4 inches per minute in hard stuff.

The drills, or "tools," are driven by steam power and special apparatus; this, however, is far too complicated to enter further into. Suffice to say, it is a most efficient apparatus, and well adapted to its purpose.

Rain Water.—The area of roofage in a brewery being very considerable, it is a question whether advantage should not be taken of it for collecting rain water, which may thus be had in large quantities. This is not the place to enter into a disquisition of the value of rain water, which is well known as the softest, and when filtered—which can be easily done at small cost—the purest; neither do we enter into the question as to its value for brewing purposes, it being well known it is not suitable; what we suggest is, the desirability of collecting it from the roofage of a brewery and using it for various purposes other than brewing to which it can be applied. For example, soft water is proved beyond a doubt the best for horses, of which of course a good number are employed about a brewery; and for washing purposes nothing can excel it. Assuming then that rain water will be valuable for more than one purpose in a brewery, we would here point out that a much larger supply of it may be obtained in the generality of cases than at first sight might be supposed, as will be seen from one or two notes at the end of this chapter.

Rain water may be stored either in underground tanks or in cisterns. A tank is strongest when made circular in section, and with an inverted bottom and arched top.

If the ground be of a soft, yielding, or treacherous character, it will be advisable to place below the bottom a layer of concrete; concrete made of broken stones, bricks, or gravel (the last is the best), and lime, five parts of the former to one of the latter, the layer of concrete being at least 12 inches thick; the bricks should be set in cement or hydraulic lime. In all cases, if a perfect job is desired, the earth should not come close up to the wall of the tank, but a space should be left between this and the earth, into which clay or puddling, as it is termed, should be hard rammed, or the space should be filled in with cement concrete. In constructing tanks of this kind, it is essential to have the brickwork carried regularly and uniformly up, no course exceeding 2 feet in height. As soon as one course is carried up all round, the puddling should be well rammed in behind the wall. When this is done up to the level of the top of the course, another course of brickwork should be carried up, and then puddled behind, and so on.

From what we have said as to the use of Portland cement concrete in the lining of wells, it need scarcely be added that it is equally advisable for building underground tanks, the construction of which in this material is somewhat similar. If the tank is to contain a large quantity of water, the form had better be rectangular, the length greater than the breadth, and the depth about equal to the breadth. The bottom should be lined with a 2-inch layer of concrete, three parts sand or crushed brick to one of Portland cement, resting upon a bottoming (see remarks upon concrete floors in first chapter) of stones 4 inches in thickness. The walls of the tank should be 9 inches thick; these are formed by a mould made by having an interior frame of wood of such dimensions that there will be 9 inches between the inside of it and the inside of the excavation; this space is filled with the concrete. The top may be arched over, or "angle irons" thrown across, clipping the walls at each side, and at 2 to 3 feet intervals; the spaces between the "angle irons" are filled in with concrete slabs, or with stones or slates.

In place of passing the rain water collected from the roof at once into the interior of the tank, it will perhaps be advisable to pass it in the first place through a small filtering tank at one end of the main tank.

The following table gives the amount of excavation in wells for each yard in depth, in cubic yards :—

Diameter of Excavation.	Quantity.	Diameter of Excavation.	Quantity.
ft. in.	cub. yards.	ft. in.	cub. yards.
3 0	·7854	7 9	5·2416
3 3	·9216	8 0	5·5851
3 6	1·0689	8 3	5·9397
3 9	1·2273	8 6	6·3051
4 0	1·3962	8 9	6·6813
4 3	1·5762	9 0	7·0686
4 6	1·7670	9 3	7·4667
4 9	1·9689	9 6	7·8759
5 0	2·1816	9 9	8·2959
5 3	2·4054	10 0	8·7267
5 6	2·6397	10 3	9·1683
5 9	2·8851	10 6	9·6210
6 0	3·1416	10 9	10·0848
6 3	3·4089	11 0	10·5594
6 6	3·6870	11 3	11·0448
6 9	3·9762	11 6	11·5410
7 0	4·2762	11 9	12·0463
7 3	4·5870	12 0	12·5664
7 6	4·9086		

The following is a table by Mr. Lowe, showing the number of gallons, &c., contained in circular tanks of different diameters, and the number of bricks required to line the excavations :—

Quantity in Gallons.	Cubic Feet.	Tons.	Depth of Tank.	Diameter of Tank.		Depth of Excavation.	Diameter of Excavation.		Cubic Yards of Excavation.	Staunching Clay in Cubic Yards.	Bricks for walls, dome, and bottom, standard size.	Total Cost.		
			ft.	ft.	in.	ft.	ft.	in.				£	s.	d.
2,269	364	11·34	10	6	10	12	9	0	28	$5\frac{2}{3}$	4,200	8	6	2
4,538	729	22·68	..	9	8	..	11	10	49	8	6,100	12	4	0
6,807	1,093	34·0	..	11	10	..	14	0	68	$10\frac{1}{4}$	7,900	15	17	4
9,076	1,458	45·36	..	13	8	..	15	10	87	$12\frac{1}{4}$	9,600	19	7	0
11,345	1,822	56·72	..	15	3	..	17	5	106	14	11,000	22	5	4
13,614	2,187	68·1	..	16	8	..	18	10	124	$15\frac{2}{3}$	12,400	25	3	6
15,883	2,551	79·4	..	18	0	..	20	2	140	$17\frac{1}{6}$	13,700	27	17	0
18,152	2,916	90·75	..	19	4	..	21	6	161	19	15,100	30	16	3
20,421	3,281	102·1	..	20	5	..	22	7	180	$20\frac{2}{3}$	16,500	33	15	0
22,690	3,645	113·4	..	21	7	..	23	9	199	22	17,900	36	3	0

The following shows areas of roofing to supply tanks of given dimensions with rain water :—

Our rainfall averages 25 inches per annum, being rather more than two cubical feet for every square foot of horizontal surface employed in catching it; or say, 200 cubical feet of water to the square. Each foot contains $6\frac{1}{4}$ gallons of water. A tank 15 feet by 9 feet × $7\frac{1}{2}$ feet, will hold 6581 gallons, and about $5\frac{1}{4}$ squares of horizontal surface would catch enough rain water to fill it in the year at the above rate of rainfall. In estimating the area of roof, the level area only must be calculated, and not the surface area, which is often half as much again. Hence the simple method is to take the area of ground plan, and double the number of feet contained in it, which will give the amount in cubical feet of water, that on the average may be collected in each year.

The following will be useful in calculating the contents of cisterns, circular in form, and of equal size top and bottom:—

Find the depth and diameter, and multiply the square by the decimal ·00285, which will find the quantity in gallons for 1 inch in depth. Multiply this by the depth, and divide by 36, and the result will be the number of barrels the cistern will hold. For each foot in depth, the number of barrels answering to the different diameters is:—

For 5 feet diameter	...	...	3·39	barrels
6 „	...	...	4·89	„
7 „	...	...	6·66	„
8 „	...	...	8·71	„
9 „	...	...	11·01	„
10 „	...	...	13·59	„

The following will enable one to determine the size of cisterns:—

The average depth of rain which falls in this latitude, although varying considerably with season and locality, rarely exceeds 7 inches for two months. The size of the cistern, therefore, in daily use, need never exceed that of a body of water on the whole roof of the building 7 inches deep.

To ascertain the amount of this, multiply the length by the breadth of the building, reduce this to inches, and divide the product by 231, and the quotient will be gallons for each inch of depth. Multiplying by seven will give the full amount for two months' rain falling upon the roof. Divide by 36, the quotient will be barrels. This will be about fourteen barrels for every surface of roof 10 feet square when measured horizontally.

Rain water may be stored in cisterns placed at some point immediately below the roof level, to admit of the water easily flowing into it. Much has been written as to the materials of which these cisterns should be made. Stone, or large slabs of slate, undoubtedly make excellent cisterns, but they are ponderous and leaky. It is to be noted, however, that stone favours the production of vegetable growth —the green algæ—while slate does not do so, at least not in such a marked manner. All stones do not, however, become equally covered with algæ in the same period, some favouring their growth more rapidly than others.

It would appear, so far as our own investigations show, that the softer the stone, the quicker does its surface become covered with algæ. But, taking everything into consideration, tanks, whether above or below ground, are best constructed of cast iron.

Galvanized iron—that is, iron coated with zinc—

has been much used in this country and in France for the making of cisterns, under the impression that there is no action upon the water contained within them. Certain circumstances having given rise to the suspicion that this opinion was not founded on fact, a French *savan*, M. Mocet, has been making investigations into the subject, and has been associated in these with M. Ancoustrant, a naval engineer. The inquiry had reference more particularly to the vessels used in the French navy for the preservation of fresh water, but, of course, bears closely upon the point before us.

The experimenters found that the zinc of galvanized iron is attacked by water; feebly in the case of distilled water, which contains little atmospheric air and carbonic acid gas; more strongly in the case of spring water, by the decomposition of the earthy carbonates, by which the carbonic acid is evolved; and strongest of all in the case of river water, which contains a notable quantity of common salt and of air. When water of the latter quality, and which is common enough, is placed in contact with galvanized iron, the quantity of carbonate and oxide of zinc created is such as to make the water highly unfit for domestic use. These, when taken into the stomach, act upon its contained acids, and create dangerous compounds, as acetate, which is astringent, nitrate, an antiseptic, and a chloride, which is caustic. In consequence of these results, the French Minister of Marine has forbidden the use of galvanized tanks for water; and enough has certainly been evolved by the inquiry to make those pause in this country who propose using this very common, and, we may say, generally esteemed metal.

Cold Liquor Back.—These backs (or tanks) are now invariably placed inside the building as near the roof as possible. Originally they were almost universally fixed outside, and formed the roof of this part of the building; this plan is, however, open to grave objection on account of the atmospheric action on the exposed water.

The capacity of the back will much depend upon circumstances—as far as the water for brewing is concerned, it need not hold more than enough for one, or at most two days' brewing. It is very advantageous to have the water pumped up fresh each day.

Sufficient head room should be left to allow for men entering to clean out same.

Cast iron is most suitable. The joints of plates should be planed, and well supported at the bottom.

The back should have the following fittings:—

Float and gauge. This latter should be fixed on a lower floor, or, where possible, near the pumps, to be easily seen.

Overflow and waste-pipe, also used as a wash-out plug. In this case the pipe should be of copper, with a gun-metal conical plug well fitted to seating of same metal. In all cases the outlet of the pipe should be visible, and *not* connected *into* any drain, to check waste, which might otherwise take place unknown.

Supply pipe to hot liquor back should have a cock fixed directly under the back to shut off in case of any accident.

Tanks in which the brewing water is to be stored are best lined with white glazed bricks set in neat Portland cement.

CHAPTER III.

ENGINES AND BOILERS.

Engines.

The Power of the engine should always be in excess of what is actually required. By this plan much loss in wear and tear is saved.

Beam Engines are sometimes used in large establishments, but are not usually recommended, on account of the number of moving parts and large first cost. The foundations are costly, and more room is taken up in the place than can always be spared.

Condensing Engines are advisable where there is plenty of water to be had at small cost, as much economy of fuel is effected in this case by their use.

The best form are horizontal, with the air-pump and condenser at the back of cylinder, and on the same bed-plate; the general design otherwise is the same as hereafter described. It is not necessary to enter here into details of this class of engines, being so seldom used in breweries.

High- and Low-pressure Engines are only recommended for large places, and when the engines are of large power. There are various forms of these, some beam engines, with the two cylinders side by side, known as "Wolf" engines, but those of the more modern type are horizontal, with the cylinders, air-pump, &c., on same bed-plate, placed one behind the other, except that the condenser usually surrounds the air-pump. We do not propose to enter into any detail as to this class of engines further than to say they are most economical as to fuel, though it is questioned by some authorities if, taking into account the great extra first cost, increased wear and tear, and the necessity for a skilled attendant, the saving is so great in the end as to render it advisable to use them, especially in a brewery, where simplicity of construction is so essential.

Horizontal Engines are the best for a brewery, all contained on one bed-plate, and with few moving parts.

Speed of Engines should not exceed 200 to 220 feet per minute of the piston, and the governors should be set to carefully regulate, to avoid accident when any apparatus or gear is thrown out of action.

Bed-plate, to which all the parts are fixed, should be substantial and of neat design, planed top and bottom, and have bolt-holes drilled.

Cylinders should be covered with felt and mahogany lagging, fixed in narrow staves, secured by brass bands, and should be fitted with steel piston and slide rods working in long gun-metal glands. Sizes above 8 H.P. should have adjustable expansion gear.

Cross Heads should be wrought iron, and the

guide blocks cast iron, or cast steel. These should be long, to prevent undue friction and cutting.

Connecting Rods.—Wrought iron polished, with gun-metal bearings at each end.

Crank Shaft.—Wrought iron, with a turned disc of cast iron well balanced, in lieu of crank.

Main Bearing should be wide and of the same size as the shaft, and be fitted with hard gun-metal.

Flywheel should be of ample size, turned on the rim and edges, boss bored out and fitted to shaft by two keys. The wheel should be carefully balanced.

Governors should be of the high-speed class, as they are the most efficient in action.

The engine should have turned bolts and studs, and shaped check-nuts fitted to all moving parts.

Steam Pipes should be clothed to prevent loss of heat and condensation. Felt may be used, or patent composition ; in any case the exterior should be kept well painted.

Condense Boxes should be fixed where necessary to keep pipes free from condensed water.

Foundations should always be most carefully constructed, as much wear and tear is saved in the working of the engines if free from vibration. All brickwork should be built in cement; the depth of same will depend upon the size of the engine and the nature of the soil.

Concrete should in all cases be placed under the brickwork and well spread beyond the foundation to assure a good base.

Base Stone should be of "hard stone," tooled all over, and rubbed, the bolt-holes drilled in same. Bolts should be of good length, and be secured by nuts and cottars, and large cast-iron plates built in the brickwork.

Engine Rooms should have stone or tile floors, and the room well ventilated; the best way is to have windows to open or close, as desirable. The room should be shut off from the brewery, and especially from the boilers, or any place where there is coal grit or dust. The walls may be decorated and varnished at a small cost, to ensure cleanliness and freedom from dust and dirt; and if all is kept in nice order, much wear and tear of the machinery will be saved, the attendant taking a personal pride in having everything neat about him.

Separate Engines.—It is advisable, in a large brewery, to use separate engines for malt rolls, pumping, cask lifting, &c. This plan saves much unnecessary wear in the shafting, economizes power, and is more convenient, especially where it may be desired to work one particular machine * or apparatus when the other part of the machinery is not wanted.

Engines should be got up bright, well painted and varnished.

Boilers.

Since the first introduction of steam, experiments have been continuously carried on to ascertain the best

* This especially applies to driving malt rolls; the speed can be better regulated.

form of boiler; the one now most commonly adopted is that known as the Cornish boiler, having an internal flue, or a tube running through the boiler according to the size. That known as the "Lancashire" boiler—from its being so largely used in that county—is a cylindrical boiler, but with two internal flues in place of one, as in the Cornish; this has been found, as a rule, when well made, one of the most economical and safe boilers in use. With a good Lancashire boiler, aided by a water-heater, one of our best authorities on boiler engineering states that he has obtained a very high result. He has evaporated as much as 10 lb. of water at 100°, by 1 lb. of coal. Fuel is economized by the introduction of Galloway's conical water-tubes into the flues, as the water circulates so much more rapidly. Carefully conducted experiments, however, would seem to show that the conical water-tube boiler "is not practically superior" to the two-flued Lancashire boiler, as "regards either evaporative economy, speed, or the prevention of smoke." There is no doubt, however, that the construction of the conical water-tubes crossing the internal flues tends greatly to strengthen the flues, and also in some measure to economize fuel by aiding the breaking up and dispersion of the current of hot air and gases as they pass along the flues. Every boiler should be fitted with one or two safety-valves, glass water-gauge, gauge-cocks, pressure-gauge, and over the furnace in the flue should be inserted a fusible plug of metal, so that in the event of the level of the water sinking below the crown of the tube, the plug would be melted, and thus an explosion be prevented. It is not desirable to cover the boiler at the top with brick-work, as in the event of any leakage going on round the manhole, &c., the boiler may be rusted through before any danger is apparent.

Multitubular Boilers are used where there is no room to set boilers in brickwork. They are very economical as to fuel, and generate steam quickly; they are best enclosed in non-conducting composition, or lagged and packed with felt.

Vertical Tubular Boilers are suitable only for small places, where there is no room for horizontal boilers. They are economical, but want skilful attention, and are not to be recommended where this cannot be had.

As the economical and safe working of boilers depends upon the care used as to certain points of management, it will serve some useful purpose if we here give a few general remarks in connection with them.

The boiler should be placed in a separate building; if not altogether detached from the main building, at least outside it. The ground upon which the furnace stands should be thoroughly well drained, and covered with concrete, so as to prevent as much as possible all damp rising up into the flues. The footings of the walls of furnace should rest upon a thick layer of Portland cement concrete, a material almost completely impervious to damp. While the boiler-house should be well ventilated, the boiler itself must be sheltered from the weather. The flues should be carefully cleaned out at regular and frequent intervals; large losses are incurred through neglect of this. The parts of the boiler exposed to the smoke should at the same time be cleaned from all adhering soot, which, together with the cleaning out of the flues, will save much coal. Where the water employed has much sediment, a cleaning apparatus should be used, in addition to blowing off occasionally, of which more hereafter.

The safety of a boiler much depends upon the mode of setting it in brickwork. All the flues should be of such dimensions as will permit of easy access to them, so that a periodical inspection of the plates may be made. This periodical, and we may add frequent inspection is of the utmost importance, as corrosion of plates from leakage may be seen, and measures taken to prevent its extension before much mischief be done. The flues should be also properly adjusted as to height, so that they may not rise above the low-water level of the boiler. A very fertile source of corrosion in the plates, and therefore of danger in the working of a boiler, is the practice of setting the boiler with a mid-feather or central longitudinal wall. This practice is one which should not be permitted where safe working of a boiler is desired. The mid-feather wall on which the central part of the boiler rests being horizontal, catches and retains any water or moisture arising from leakage, and rapidly hastens corrosion of the plates. But another source of danger arises from this mode of setting boilers, causing a change of form in the plates at that part where the boiler rests upon the mid-feather—this change causes the plates to be flattened, and in some cases to such a degree that the position of the mid-feather wall can be distinctly traced inside the boiler. This changing action varies with the varying pressure in the boiler, and tends to strain the "ring seams" of the rivets, and make them leak, and this accelerates the corrosion of the plates. Boilers should be set on two lines of fire lumps, with side and bottom flues.

Further, let the boiler be of ample dimensions; it is most mistaken economy to have small boiler power; it is cheaper to use a boiler considerably in excess of the engine power than to work one only equal to it or a little more.

The chimney-stalk should be of such dimensions as will ensure a good draught, the amount of this being in excess rather than the reverse. By the judicious use of the damper, where an excess of draught is arranged for, the boiler can be worked more economically; for if the draught is only strong enough to meet the demands of ordinary circumstances, we have obviously no power to draw upon when we wish to work more efficiently or quickly; we must therefore fall back upon rapid firing and free use of coals—a bad practice.

It is obviously not the province of the present work to enter into a disquisition as to what constitutes good and safe construction in a boiler; to ensure this as far as possible is doubtless the interest, as it should be the object of the purchaser, and he, as a rule, is compelled to trust to the maker he employs, or the professional man whom he consults. But there are points in the management of a boiler, and appliances attached to, or which should be attached to it, the overlooking of which, in order that they be attended to by the men employed, is within the province of the employer or his manager, and which therefore demand the best exercise of his attention and care. To some of these points and appliances mention has been made in a very general way in the introduction to the present chapter; but we now give, in connection with them, a few more special remarks and suggestions.

The first point of importance in the management of a boiler to be attended to is the supply of water. This is all-essential; for no matter what the complete nature of the other appliances to ensure safety may be, these will be rendered nugatory if the water is not supplied to it in proper quantity and at a proper time. The attention, therefore, of the engineer must always unceasingly be paid to see to this being secured. The working of the pump which supplies the boiler should be seen to, for it often happens that it may be apparently working and yet the valves may be sticking, or some other cause may prevent it drawing water, and thus to all appearance working well, and yet be sending no water into the boiler. To know how a pump is working, it should in all cases be provided with a small stop-cock on the pipe which leads the water from the pump to the boiler and towards the boiler side of the pump-pipe. By opening this cock, it will be at once seen whether water is being passed through the pipe or not; if no water is forced through the opened cock the pump is not working; this may arise from two causes: first, the valves or clacks may be sticking in the seats; to loosen them the pump may be struck with a wooden mallet at the part where the valves are seated. This will generally start the valves and cause them to act, rising and falling with the upward and downward action of the pump-plunger. The second cause may arise from the plunger fitting so loosely that it draws air, and therefore does not form the vacuum properly; this may be set right for the time by passing some water into the pump through the stuffing-box, which will probably make the pump draw water properly, which will be made evident by opening the cock formerly described. Another way of supplying water to boilers is by the injector. This singular apparatus—for its working is almost paradoxical, and has given rise to all sorts of theories to account for its action—is now almost universally used in locomotives and in other forms of boilers. It possesses this great advantage, that it works with a very small pressure of steam in the boiler; but it will not work where water is employed above the temperature of 120°, the best temperature being 60°; and further, it will usually not draw water from a greater depth than 6 feet. The force-pump and the injector then, being possessed of disadvantages, the "donkey engine," as it is called, is rising in favour. This, as some of our readers may not be aware, is a small separate steam-engine, the duty of which is merely to pump the water into the boiler. Very successful have these engines been, as they are capable of drawing water from the full practicable depth influenced by the vacuum and at a high temperature, and when out of order are easily repaired. Still they have at the best been so comparatively complicated in their parts, that their consequent cost has kept many from using them. Recently, however, several firms have introduced forms of donkey engines which, for simplicity of construction, and from the ease with which they are set to and kept at work, and also from the ease with which they are repaired, are nearly all that can be desired for supplying boilers with water. They can be set to work also with a pressure of steam in the boiler as low as 15 lb. to the square inch; and by merely giving a larger cylinder, or using the next size to that required to do certain work, as low a pressure as 10 lb. steam can be used.

But to ensure the safe working of steam boilers, not only is it necessary that we should have the means of supplying the boiler with water, but we should also *have the means of knowing* when that supply is deficient, when over-abundant, or when of proper quantity. The appliances which are designed to give the attendant this information are very numerous; those chiefly used being known by the names of gauge-cocks, water-gauges, water or float indicators. In the case of "gauge-" cocks as fixed to a boiler, when one tap is opened and steam issues from it, and when the other tap is open and water issues from it, the condition of the boiler, so far as its supply of water is concerned, is considered to be right. This is the theory of the action of the apparatus, but practice materially modifies it, and introduces an element of danger too frequently overlooked even by practised engineers. It is this, that in opening the two taps water may issue from both of them, thus indicating that too much water is in the boiler; or on opening the steam-tap steam may issue from it, and water from the water-tap, thus indicating the right condition of water; yet the supply of water may be dangerously low, even below the level of the water-tap. This will be caused by "priming," by which term is meant that condition of steam in which a large quantity of water is carried up by it above the level of the water; so that water or watery steam may be blown out of the water-tap, while in reality the water is far below the pipe. This may happen at any time, and therefore renders the arrangement of gauge-cocks now described anything but trustworthy guides or indicators of the internal condition of the boiler. Another appliance is therefore used—the "water-gauge glass." This is an absolutely necessary appliance to a boiler; great care should be taken that the gauge glass is kept clean and bright, so that its action can be easily seen. It is a good plan to have two of these gauges, by which an indication of one can be read off against the other.

Another apparatus connected with the water supply to a boiler, and by means of which the level of the water in the boiler is shown, is the "float" indicator, with its well-known wheel and counterpoise weight. This is, however, apt to become deranged through the sticking of the float rod in its stuffing-box. To prevent this as much as possible, the attendant should frequently examine the apparatus, and work the rod up and down the stuffing-box.

We now turn our attention to the steam fittings connected with the safety of boilers—the first of which in importance is the "safety-valve," often safety but in name. In all reports drawn up on the working of steam boilers in this country, to no point is reference more frequently made than to the danger arising from neglect of safety-valves; they are found overweighted, even in some gross instances tied down, to prevent them rising; they are left in such a dirty, neglected condition that the valves stick in their seats, or the lever is so dirty or rusted that it will not work in the joints; all these elements of danger can be got rid of by the exercise of attention and care, and which should be insisted upon by all employers and managers. To prevent all tampering with the weights on a safety-valve, two should be provided, one locked up. But although a properly adjusted safety-valve indicates by its blowing off at a given pressure the amount of that pressure, still it affords no indication of the pressure of steam in the boiler at points below this pressure, or at points above it, should anything have gone wrong to prevent the safety-valve acting at the pressure for which it was adjusted. It is absolutely necessary to have a "steam-gauge" attached to the boiler. This is sometimes attached to the pipe near the engine, but the vibration from this affects the gauge, and of course its indications.

Boilers are frequently affected in their economical working, and also in their safety, by incrustation arising from matter deposited from the water. Water varies much in the percentage of matter contained in it, liable to be deposited. Some waters are very bad, necessitating frequent cleaning out of the boiler. The usual way to get rid of deposited matters before they become fixed, or incrusted to the boiler plates, is to blow off the water from time to time by the pressure of the steam. Care should be taken to fit up the blow-off pipes and valves so as to ensure not only their efficient working, but to prevent leakage. If cocks or taps be used, they should be wholly of gun metal, as cocks of combined metal, or brass plugs and cast-iron shells, are liable to go wrong through unequal expansion. When made entirely of gun metal, and fitted with glands and carefully packed, they may be relied on. Blowing off, where the water used contains much sedimentary matter, and where the ordinary blow-off apparatus is used, should be done at regular intervals during the day, and while the engine is not at work. At these times the water is more quiescent, and the matter is thus allowed to settle. A very capital contrivance for getting rid of the deposited matter in water is by the use of the cleaning or "scum-pipe." This has been long used with marine boilers; it has only recently been applied to land boilers, but with such success, that in some instances where they were coated in the course of a month or six weeks with a heavy deposit without the scum-pipe, they were found, at the end of the same period, perfectly clean with it. The following is Mr. Fletcher's description of it:—"The description of pipe adopted is about three or four inches in diameter, having a wing cast on each side so as to form a trough throughout the entire length of the pipe. This pipe is carried within the boiler from one end to the other, being made in any convenient lengths for introduction at the manhole. On the top it is perforated longitudinally with small holes, the aggregate area of the whole number of the holes being equal to that of the pipe itself. The top of the trough is placed a few inches below water level, so that the scum may flow over it; when, being guarded from disturbance by ebullition, it deposits in the still water above the trough the sedimentary particles held by it in mechanical combination. By means of a tap which communicates with the scum-pipe, and which is fixed to the front-end plate of the boiler, the deposit may be blown out as often as necessary, which should be about every two hours during ebullition. The tap should be about two inches in diameter, made entirely of brass, fitted with a gland, and having a wrought-iron waste-pipe attached. The waste-pipes from the glass water-gauges may be connected with it, being led directly under the dead-plate, which makes a compact arrangement. The most convenient place to fix the scum-pipe is at the side of the boiler rather than in the centre, as in the latter position it is more easily fixed, and offers less obstruction to getting inside the boiler. The foregoing scum-pipe is simple in construction, and affords a large collecting area."

But although the incrustation can be greatly prevented by blowing out in the ordinary way, or by the use of the "scum-pipe," it cannot in some waters be completely so; in these the use of soda in the boiler is highly recommended. When used, however, it should be along with a scum-pipe, as otherwise "priming" is caused, in consequence of the foam produced in the boiling water, through the combination of the soda with the grease contained in the water.

The following is a method of introducing the soda into the boiler:—"A small vessel, capable of containing about two gallons of water, is placed on the suction portion of the water-pipe by which the boiler is supplied, and a pipe of half an inch in diameter communicates from the water-pipe to this vessel. Every day the boiler-man puts into this vessel from one to one and a half pounds of soda ash. In feeding the boiler, the fireman turns the small cock, when in three or four minutes all the solution is taken up and passed through the feed-pump. This is repeated daily, and the consequence is that not the slightest incrustation is formed."

Boilers are often weakened through the overheating of the plates, this arising from matter becoming deposited, and preventing the contact of the water with the plates. This evil we have treated of under the head of our remarks on incrustation; but it is worthy of being noted here, that overheating is frequently caused by the matter deposited from greasy water—the grease owing its presence to the practice, pretty frequently carried out, of passing the exhaust steam of the engine to a tank or cistern containing water, for the purpose of heating, before passing it into the boiler.

Feed-water Heater.—Much economy results from the use of an apparatus of this kind; there are many in successful use; the mode of working is, however, about the same in all.

Tubular Heaters consist of an outer cylinder, provided with an upper and lower chamber, connected by a number of small tubes. The outer chamber contains the feed water, exhaust steam being passed through the tubes; much of the earthy and other matters in the water are deposited, and nearly pure water only enters the boilers. The amount of steam to be admitted is regulated to suit the heat of water required.

Plain Cylindrical Heaters are close cylinders into which feed water is admitted; the exhaust steam being blown on to the surface of the water, the excess of steam passes away. These are very simple, and are nearly as economical as the above.

In supplying boilers with feed water, it is a usual plan to admit the water at the lower part of the boiler. This plan is objectionable on account of the strain it throws on the bottom lines of the rivets, through the contraction of the plates, more especially when the water is cold. The plan recommended by the Manchester Boiler Association obviates this and other disadvantages. It consists in supplying the feed water at a high level, near the surface of the water in fact. The vertical pipe supplying the water is placed in front of the boiler, and provided at top with a feed-box with stop-valve and wheel within easy reach of the fireman; a horizontal pipe is connected with the feed-box, and is passed into the interior of the boiler at the level of or near to the surface of the water. The pipe is provided with a series of perforations, through which the water passes to the interior of the boiler.

Stoking.—One of the most important points connected with the economical working of boilers is the management of the fuel; in other words, the "stoking" or "firing-up." One good rule, if not the only and the best, to ascertain whether there is good stoking, is to watch from time to time the state of matters at the top of the chimney-stalk. If from this issues dense volumes of black smoke, it may be set down as a safe decision that the stoking is bad, and the fuel wasted. We speak of furnaces, of course, in which there are no special appliances adapted for the "consumption of smoke," as the phrase goes. Appliances of this sort are endless; but experience has long convinced us that prevention of smoke is better than its consumption—if that be the right term—when produced; and of all smoke preventers, there is nothing so efficient as good stoking. A few words as to what stoking is may not be here out of place.

There are three modes of stoking—the first, in which the coals are spread over the surface from the bridge gradually up to the "dead-plate." This is the ordinary method, and when carelessly done causes much smoke, which rises rapidly, and issues from the stalk in black, dense volumes. When properly done, however, and with the precaution of having a banked-up heap of red-hot fuel at the bridge, little smoke comparatively is produced. A good deal depends upon the size of the fuel employed in this kind of stoking. With slack or very small coal, it is the only mode by which quick evaporation can be secured. The mode presently described as "caking" firing being too slow in this respect, in this kind of stoking, to obtain the best results, it is necessary to have the fuel as uniform in size as possible. Mixed coal, with large lumps and small combined, makes the very worst coal to fire with. The next point to be attended to is to fire evenly, regularly, and frequently. Watt's instruction to stokers may be quoted here :—"The oftener you fire, and the thinner, the better. The fire should be kept an equal thickness, and free from open places or holes, which are extremely prejudicial, and should be filled up as soon as they appear."

The "caking" method of stoking is to heap up the coals on the dead-plate at the front of the furnace, allowing the mass to cake, the gases being gradually evolved; when the upper part is thoroughly caked and a mass of red-hot fuel, it is pushed towards the bridge, and a fresh supply of coal put on the dead-plate. This system does best with round coal.

Management of the Engine.—Much cannot be said here, as this would involve going into so many technical details, not easily communicated in a brief space, and which, moreover, are not within the province of our work to discuss. The few words we have to give will obviously therefore be of a very general nature. At the outset we would strongly recommend one thing to be done as a point of the truest economy, and that is, employ a properly trained and skilled mechanic. Let it be remembered that both the boiler and the engine make together a very complicated and costly mechanism, the bad working of which may, and will almost surely result in waste of money and of time, which in a large concern is a matter of some moment; to which may be added the serious consideration, that upon their proper management rests the security of life and property with which they are surrounded; it is a mistake to suppose that any man is fit to take charge of an engine and boiler, and one that has occasioned no small loss. Having done the best to secure the services of a well-qualified man, the good test of his work after a little service will be to watch the regular condition of his engine and boiler-house, and the external appearance of their various parts. If, as a rule, he has everything well ordered and "natty" about him, the houses clean, and nothing lying about in disorder, the polished parts of the engine and boiler clean and bright, it may be set down that he is attentive to his business, and worth his wages—which, parenthetically, we may put here, should be good, for the man who is careful in these things, and they are in themselves very important, is almost sure to be equally so in seeing that all the appliances and working parts of his boiler and engine are in good order. As far as the engine is concerned, a master or manager, in ordinary circumstances, is not expected to know, unless he is technically acquainted with the details of mechanical engineering, whether the engine is giving out its fullest and most economical power; but there is one point he can observe, and its observation will often save money, and that is, if the engine works noisily, the parts jarring and knocking, he may rest assured there is something wrong. It may be taken as an axiom in mechanics that all noise and jar in the working of any machine is evidence of its being out of order somewhere.

Furnaces for Smoke Consuming.—The oldest and best furnace for large boilers or coppers is "Juckes'," which consists of an endless chain of bars worked by machinery. It is self-feeding. The coal is carried forward to the bridge, and slowly burned before any smoke is made. In the large breweries as many as twenty-five of these are at work at one place. The economy in fuel effected is considerable.

There are many modifications of the above, but none that give such satisfactory results in working.

"**Wright's**" furnace is inexpensive and very efficient as far as prevention of smoke is concerned, but no economy of fuel results.

There are numerous others; we do not, however, propose to enter further into the matter.

CHAPTER IV.

MACHINERY AND GEAR.

Transmitting Motion.—Leather bands are usually the best, especially where there is not much waste steam in the place; the power can be transmitted some distance and at small expense, with very little loss from "friction."

Ropes have been used for this purpose in mills, but we do not recommend their use in a brewery.

Wheel gear is another plan, special details of which are noted at page 53.

In large breweries, as before named, we advise the use of several engines, by which means much shafting and gear is saved, and great economy in working is also effected.

Duplicates should be kept of all the principal parts in case of a break-down. All wheels, pulleys, &c., should be bored to standard gauge, with same dimensions of keys, to suit their respective shafts.

All special machines and apparatus are described hereafter in separate chapters.

We now give some important particulars, as to details of driving gear, &c.

Shafting should be turned all over, to enable extra wheels to be keyed on at any time; it should be to "standard gauge," and all wheels, pulleys, and bosses of any kind bored out to same; in case of accident a wheel, &c., can be renewed at any time, and be sure to fit.

All couplings should be of the flanged kind, faced, turned, and holes drilled. The bearings same size as shaft, and should not be more than 7 feet centres for 2 inch, 8 feet 6 inches for 3 inch, 10 feet for 4 inch.

Collars on shafts should have countersunk steel screws recessed in the shaft, with square, not conical points.

Pulleys should be turned on the rims and edges, and should be well rounded to save the straps cutting; they should be at least 1 inch wider than the belt, and coned on the periphery to give a grip to same.

Tooth Wheel Gear.—The iron pinion wheel should be pitched and trimmed, and the face and edges of teeth turned. The wheel it gears into should be a "mortise" wheel, fitted with wood cogs, made of hornbeam, apple, or beech; the wood must be well seasoned, and none used under four years old. The teeth must fit close, so as to avoid "back lash" and uneven working.

Disengaging Gear.—The various parts of the shafting are usually thrown out of gear by the following apparatus:—

When continuous, by clutches with levers as de scribed.

When at some distance from the "driver," and driven by belts, by fast and loose pulleys.

Cone clutches are occasionally used where any shafting is required to be thrown into gear while running.

Most machines, &c., are thrown in and out of gear by clutches.

Clutch Levers should have gun-metal "nogs" working on steel pins, and the lever should always be secured in a quadrant by pin or bolt to save accident when in or out of gear; in some cases, it is advisable that the levers should be locked, to prevent any unqualified person interfering with same.

Lubricators should be attached to each bearing, with oil cups or catchers below to save dirt and loss of oil.

Plummer Blocks should have wide gun-metal bearings, be planed on the bases, and all bolts should have check nuts.

Wall Boxes should be planed for base of the plummer block, and a space or pocket below to allow of removal of bolts.

Wall Brackets should be substantial, and be well bolted to the walls; where possible the bolts should pass through the wall.

Lubricants.—Good mineral oil is the best and cheapest; vegetable oil is not good; and lard oil, never very suitable, should not be used, owing to the difficulty in getting the same pure.

Where shafting passes through waste steam places it should be painted, in other parts it should be kept clean and bright.

CHAPTER V.

MALT MILLS.

THERE has been little alteration in the form of malt mills during the last few years, the plan for moderate-sized rolls being to have two of equal size of steel, or of cast iron of a close hard texture. We have used them of chilled cast iron, but the extra expense of bringing them to a true surface is hardly compensated by the extra wear. Some brewers prefer having the rolls self-adjusting, by means of springs or weights instead of screws, with the idea of permitting any hard foreign substance which may have found its way into the malt to pass between the rolls without causing damage; in practice there is little real advantage in such an arrangement; in the first place, if the rolls are fitted, as they should be, with a strong screen, there is no chance of anything large enough to do any damage reaching or passing through the rolls; and in the next place, for large and heavy rolls to do their proper work, the springs (or weights) require to be so strong or heavy that the rolls are fixed almost as rigidly as where screws are employed. For light rolls it is not of much consequence; but heavy ones drive more regularly by being geared together. For rolls to grind perfectly, they should be set to just crack each grain without crushing them. When we consider how various are the sizes of the grains, it is obvious, without some special arrangement, one pair of rollers cannot do this. Several schemes have been proposed: one, for instance, having three sets of rollers mounted in one frame, then, by rather a complicated arrangement of screens, the malt is divided into the three divisions, each size of malt finding its way to its proper pair. We have introduced a much cheaper arrangement, and which answers every purpose, viz. by having a double screen, one fine, the other of a coarser mesh. The rolls are set for the large-size malt, the smaller particles falling into a separate hopper. When a sufficient quantity has collected, the rolls are adjusted to suit, and the smaller-sized malt is ground. In order that the malt should be well ground, the rolls should run at an even and regular speed. To obtain this in large breweries, it is generally desirable to have a special separate engine for driving the malt rolls, as when driven from the main engine the grinding is continually being interrupted by the engine being slackened or stopped, to throw one or other of the various machines in or out of gear. If a separate engine, however, cannot be introduced, it is a good arrangement to have the feed regulated with a governor driven from the spindle of one of the rolls, so that, according to the speed at which the rolls are running, so the malt is passed to them.

Screens.—Every set of rolls should be provided with a good screen. There are several descriptions of screens now in use, which have quite superseded the old kind, in which the wires are secured to the bearers by binding wire, and which are continually giving way. One of the most durable kind is that in which each individual wire is turned round each bearing bar, so that the screen must remain good until the wires themselves are worn through. A screen of this description also presents a very even surface for the malt to pass over, and can be laid at a less angle than one of the ordinary kind.

Screens are generally better fixed, but where there is not sufficient space to get proper angle, say 45°, they are made movable, and are driven by gear from the rolls.

The screens should be enclosed, and provided with a dirt and dust box; it is advisable to have the enclosure made of hard wood, and polished for the sake of cleanliness.

Malt or Grain Measurers.—A very valuable machine in a brewery is a good and accurate malt measurer. One which answers its purpose thoroughly was patented some twenty years ago by Mr. King. The machine is extremely simple, consisting of a hollow cylinder containing one quarter; this cylinder is divided into eight compartments, each gauged to hold one bushel; therefore for every revolution of the cylinder a quarter of malt is measured and duly registered; there is an index fixed on the axle of the cylinder, which index being locked up prevents the men in charge tampering with the machine. In the event of the supply of grain or malt ceasing, a valve is so arranged that it closes, and in closing, by means of a lever, throws the band off the driving pulley and stops the machine until such time as sufficient grain has collected to open the valve again, when the belt is thrown on to the fast rigger, and the machine is once more set going.

This machine has now (1880) stood the test of about twenty years' work; it is used in all the principal London breweries, it is most efficient in action, and when once adjusted it is impossible to have an error in registration.

Another useful machine has been patented by W. Baxter, and which has proved a reliable grain-weighing machine. It is capable of weighing and registering at the rate of 10 tons per hour. The machine consists of a cylinder divided into compartments, and hung on one end of a lever; on the other end (which is graduated) is hung a weight. By means of a simple arrangement, when a sufficient weight of grain is placed in the upper compartment of the cylinder, so as to overcome the weight on the lever, the cylinder makes a partial revolution, emptying the loaded compartment, and bringing the next one into use, each revolution being registered on a dial.

CHAPTER VI.

MALT AND GRIST CONVEYORS.

THE usual method employed for raising malt or grist is by a "Jacob's ladder" or elevator, the best form of which is to have the case of cast iron, the head fitted with brasses for the spindle of top pulley to work in; the lower end fitted with brasses, and adjusting screws for tightening the belt, which should be of leather, the width, of course, depending upon the quantity of malt or grist to be conveyed. The buckets should be made either of tin or of light galvanized iron, and may be attached to the belt either by screws, rivets, or, if of tin, by tin keys. The "Jacobs" are best driven from the top; if driven from the bottom, the belt to which the buckets are attached must be kept much tighter. There should be convenient doors in the case for examining the buckets and tightening the belt, &c., and a door at the bottom for convenience of cleaning out. "Jacobs" should be fitted with a very light door or valve at the top, in case of the dust which always more or less hangs about the "case" catching fire. When first expense is an object, "Jacobs" do very well with the legs of the case made of wood instead of iron as above described.

For conveying malt or grist laterally or horizontally from one place to another on the same level, an "Archimedean screw" is the best arrangement, the screw being made with a cast-iron centre shaft, with ribs cast on to suit the pitch of the screw, and blades of light sheet iron are riveted to these ribs. The case should be of iron, and the bearings in which the axis of the screw works may either be secured to side, or better still, from the top or cover of the case. In the latter instance, the bearings are much more easily adjusted. All the bearings should be fitted with lubricators. It is a very effectual way of screening malt to have the first length of screws either perforated with small holes or constructed of stout iron wire. It will generally be found advantageous to have the last two or three feet of the cover of the screw case made as light as possible, so that if by any chance the delivery of the screw gets choked, the cover is forced off and the grain is thrown out, and so prevents any damage to the screw.

Another method of conveying grain, much used in large warehouses, is by means of an endless band, and by the employment of an adjustable stop the grain or malt can be delivered at any part of the house required, the speed of the belt being about 200 feet per minute.

CHAPTER VII.

MASH TUNS AND MACHINES.

Mash Tuns are, as a rule, constructed of wood—oak staves and Dantzic timber bottoms—in breweries where ale is the principal production; but where porter and stout are brewed, and where a little additional expense, in the first instance, is not objected to, then iron mash tuns are very generally adopted. From an engineering point of view, iron tuns possess many advantages, the principal are the ease with which they are cleaned out, and the surface being smooth there are no cracks for wort to lodge in and become acid. Whether or not the iron acts injuriously upon the "wort" is a brewers' question, which it is not within our province to discuss.

Mash tuns have been used of cast iron with a lining of copper; steam is admitted in the annular space to keep the mash hot; they are very cleanly, but costly as to first outlay.

There have been many patents taken out for keeping the contents of the tun hot whilst mashing, &c. The best form for an iron tun, which has given considerable satisfaction where we have advised their erection, is to have the bottom of the tun cast hollow, allowing a steam space of about 1½ inch. This arrangement is very simple, and cannot get out of order, and the tun can be as easily cleaned as an ordinary one. All iron tuns should be cased on the outside either with felt or suitable material to retain the heat.

Where there is height it is a great convenience to have a valve fitted in the bottom of the tun for getting the grains out, so saving the labour required for throwing the grains over the edge of the tun, as is usually done.

If the grains cannot be dropped direct into carts, an endless band can be used to convey them to a receiving tank. To check the quantity delivered to each person, a measuring apparatus of simple construction is attached to the shoot from the tank.

False bottoms can be made either of cast iron, copper, or gun metal, with drilled holes or slots, the latter giving the largest amount of drainage; but as the slots should not exceed $\frac{1}{20}$ inch in width, very great care is required in the manufacture of such plates. Copper bottoms have the slots cut out by a punch, after which the plates are planished.

Spargers work best with three arms, and should be constructed to revolve freely and be well balanced, so as to work regularly. The arms should be attached by screws to centre cup, and the ends fitted with caps and screws to allow of cleaning out.

Mashing machines may be divided into three classes — self-acting external machines, external machines that require driving, and internal machines.

For small tuns an external machine is all that is required, as with some of the self-acting machines a perfect mash can be effected of any required consistency. Of the external mashing machines requiring driving "Steel's" has had the greatest success; another, patented by Sorrel, has this advantage—that as it consists of three chambers, each fitted with rakes, it allows the use of two liquors of different temperatures, introducing that of the lowest degree in the first chamber where the grist enters the machine, and that of the highest degree in the third or last chamber. Willison's Patent Machine is an apparatus that can be used with much advantage, especially as it is self-acting, and does not require any power to drive. It is simple and efficient in action, being fitted with internal "rakes"; it prevents "balling," and makes a thorough mash. It has been successfully worked for some years.

For a large mash tun it is desirable to erect an internal machine. If the tun is not of great depth one rake shaft will be sufficient; but if over 5 feet deep the machine should be fitted with two rake shafts, and should also be arranged with fast and slow motion and reversing gear, so as to be able to drive the machine either way round the tun. The rakes patented by P. R. Conron are the most effective that can be used, the patent consisting in fitting to the end of each rake a strip of indiarubber of sufficient length to just touch the false bottom plates. By the use of these rakes it is possible to mash with grist ground much finer than by any other kind, as in consequence of the indiarubber touching the plates every revolution the holes are cleared, and a good drainage is secured.

Internal machines are best driven from the bottom, which keeps the upper part of tun clear from all obstructions.

Covers to Mash Tuns.—In the large breweries tuns are covered over by copper covers, raised and lowered by machinery or counterbalance gear, and in other places the top is of wood, either fixed close to top of tun with flaps to open, or say 3 feet above top with side shutters to slide. It is, however, preferable to keep the cover as close as possible to the top of the tun to retain the heat of mash.

CHAPTER VIII.

PUMPING APPARATUS.

Although many kinds of patent pumps have been put before the public, in our opinion the best for a brewery are the three-throw "lift pumps." The barrels should be made of gun metal, with gun-metal buckets and copper rods; the valves of the same material, and either of the flap or spindle kind—we prefer the latter. The lift of the valves should be carefully adjusted. Top and bottom valve boxes should be cast iron, with separate chambers and valves to each pump. Bonnets and "hand holes" should be supplied at each valve. Suction and delivery pipes are best of copper, with flanges or unions to disconnect readily. It should be borne in mind all parts of a set of pumps should be easily accessible in case of stoppage from any cause.

The speed of pumps should not exceed for 2 inches diameter, 35 strokes per minute; 3 inches, 30; 4 inches, 25; 6 inches, 18. For well pumps, the speed must be arranged according to depth.

We do not usually advise pumps larger in diameter than 6 inches (except in very large places), but prefer to increase the number of sets of pumps, always taking care to have spare pumps in case of accident or break-down.

Crank Shafts should be wrought iron or steel, and the pins about same diameter as the other part. Connecting rods should be wrought iron, with fork ends fitted with gun-metal bearings, gibs, and keys. Cross-heads wrought iron.

The pumps are usually fixed to side frames, with proper guides attached. As to the means of driving, belts or geared wheels can be used; but where there is not much waste steam about the place, belts are preferable.

On the "rising main" should be fixed a good copper air vessel of ample capacity. By this means a continuous flow of liquor or wort is ensured. A draw-off cock should be fitted in same, to renew the air from time to time; otherwise they are useless, as the air becomes absorbed.

Well Pumps.—The pumps should be made in much the same way as above described, except that some modifications are necessary for deep lifts, or for cases where the pumps are sunk below the water level. In this instance, the rising main of each pump is a continuation of the barrels, and the top valve box is fixed above the water; this enables the delivery valves to be examined, or the buckets to be drawn, without regard to the water level. The kind of valves depends much upon the depth of well and "head" to be pumped; in any case, metal valves should be used. For large pumps, double-beat valves, on the "Cornish" plan, are the best, but are rather expensive. There are many kinds of valves used for deep well pumping, but the subject is too large to enter upon here.

The pumps should work slow, to enable the valves to close at each stroke.

Cranks should be of wrought iron, or, where expense is not an object, they should be of steel. The top framing should be wrought iron where possible, and the bearings of shaft long, and made of hard gun metal or phosphor bronze.

Eccentrics can be used for small depths, say to 50 feet. The shafts should be of wrought iron, and the straps of eccentrics either gun metal or cast iron lined with same.

Tooth wheels are the best for driving; wood and iron teeth pitched and trimmed.

The air vessel should be large and easily got at, with gear from the top to drain same and admit air when required. It must be borne in mind (as before named) air is absorbed by the water, and in a short time, if the vessel is not re-charged with air, the apparatus is useless.

Delivery Pipes should be of ample size, and all bends of easy curve, and fitted with an air cock to open occasionally to discharge the air.

We have not entered into details as to pump rods and guides, &c., as these vary with each case, and must always be left in professional hands.

Double-action Pumps are sometimes used, but as

they are more complicated to keep in repair, we do not advise their use for brewery work.

Centrifugal Pumps are not suitable for high lifts, the amount of power required to work same being great.

Steam Pumps.—These may be divided into two classes: First, those worked by "tappet motion"; second, those worked by flywheel.

The former give much trouble, and, as a rule, are constantly out of repair.

The last-named are very useful where pumping has to be done at a distance from the shafting. We have used in many places with much satisfaction the "Model pump" made by Thornewill and Warham, Burton-on-Trent. The whole of the apparatus is self-contained, the parts well proportioned, with good arrangements for examination of valves, &c. They are far more economical in the use of steam than the "tappet pumps," and are not likely to get out of order.

One of these pumps with barrel 4 inches diameter will discharge seventy-five barrels per hour.

Pulsometer.—This singular instrument is sometimes used with advantage as a temporary pump in well sinking; they do not require any fixing. They are not, however, suitable for permanent work in breweries.

CHAPTER IX.

HOISTING MACHINERY.

There are various kinds of labour to be performed in a brewery or malting where machinery can be introduced with great advantage; and as this subject is a large one, we propose to describe the most modern appliances for such purposes.

1st. Steam Power.—For raising malt, hops, &c., sack tackle gear is most usually employed. There are several ways of working these; we herein describe the most effective.

Barrel Gear, worked by tight and loose strap, with brake-wheel and brake. In this case, the driving strap runs over flanged pulleys, and is thrown in and out of gear by a lever fitted with a roller at the end, to tighten strap. It can also be arranged to work the brake at same time, if required.

Barrel worked by "Cones."—In this case the barrel has cones attached, with sliding cone clutches, provided with lever to throw in and out of gear. The brake is worked by same lever, and gear is attached to stop machinery at the highest point. The barrel runs loose upon the shaft, the cone clutches working upon a feather key, so that when thrown in the barrel revolves with the shaft. Great care must be taken in proportioning the size and angle of the "cones," otherwise much trouble will take place; but when properly constructed, they are both simple and efficient in action. When brakes are attached, the same lever that works the cones also controls the brakes, and can be made self-acting.

Barrel Gear, worked by patent frictional gear, is very simple, silent in working, and most effective. The shaft carrying the barrel in this case runs in eccentric bushes or bearings connected together, and by means of a lever is brought into contact with the driving grooved wheel, which throws in and out of gear and puts on the brake at same time. Self-acting striking gear is attached, to stop at highest point.

Steam Hoists.—When the shafting is at some distance, special steam hoists can be used. As the design of these is very numerous, and to suit special cases, it would be out of the province of this book to enter further into the matter.

Jacob or Elevator.—When large quantities of grain in bulk have to be unloaded at the water-side, a special arrangement is made of this apparatus; the angle and height of same is capable of adjustment, and the steam power is made portable. As this, however, is a somewhat complicated apparatus, and cannot well be described without the aid of drawings, we merely notice it.

2nd. Hydraulic Apparatus.—When a large

amount of work is to be done, especially at a long distance from the boiler power, this is the best apparatus to be employed. There are two methods of working same:

1st. Head of water from a tank at highest point of the place, and by Town's pressure from the mains (where the authorities will permit its use).

2nd. Water pumped under pressure and stored in an "accumulator."

No. 1 Plan—Low Pressure.—Lifts for raising casks can be worked by fall of water from the liquor back or any tank fixed at the highest point in the place, and are self-acting, the water being pumped up at any convenient time when the engines are not doing any other work. They are constructed on two plans:

Ram Lifts.—The platform or table to carry goods, working between two T-iron or cast-iron guides, with planed faces, is fixed to a hollow ram (or piston) working in a cylinder, sunk in the ground, fitted with stuffing-box, the depth of this being equal to the height lifted.

Valve motion admits the water into the cylinder under the ram, and so raises the weight. It is also arranged to stop and lower the platform as required, and by a self-acting gear stops at the highest and lowest points.

The great advantages of this plan are, absolute safety, easy and silent working, and very little wear and tear.

They can be made to lift any height, which is convenient where beer has to be raised from a deep cellar, or where it is to be stored, as in some London breweries, where space is valuable, upon an upper floor.

For "loading out" they are usefully employed, the platform in this case rising to the level of the dray or cart.

For spirit and wine they are the most suitable, owing to the great value of the goods and the absolute safety of the apparatus.

Short-stroke Cylinders (with gear, or movable pulleys, &c).—On this plan, the platform and guides with the valve motion remain as before. The power to work the lift is applied thus:—Cylinder with piston or ram with stroke equal to, say, one-third (or less) the height to be lifted, and by means of chains running over movable pulleys, conducted to top pulley fixed over the platform, the weight is raised. This plan is not so safe as the other, but is less costly in construction, although the wear and tear is much more.

Crane Jibs are also worked by this plan, and in many cases are more convenient for "loading out," as the cask can be put direct into the dray, and so saves labour.

There are many other uses to which this plan can be applied, but as it would occupy too much space to go into such a large question, we have given the leading features only.

No. 2 Plan—High Pressure.—Lifts as before described are worked both by "ram" and the short cylinders, and also crane jibs for small or great heights.

The power is given by pumping water into an "accumulator," which is a loaded ram working in a cylinder somewhat like an hydraulic press. The required pressure is given by weights in a casing fixed to top of ram, and varies from 200 to 750 lb. per square inch.

All the parts are very powerful, and lifting can be done as easily and as safely upon this plan as the other.

It is suitable where several lifts and cranes have to be worked, and especially where the *boiler power is some distance away.* The pressure pipes in this case are carried either under the ground or above, according to convenience. They can be used in fire-proof places, and (unlike steam pipes) do not affect the temperature or give trouble by leakage. We do *not* advise this plan for small places, or where there is to be only one or two lifts, &c., as it would not pay, taking into account the cost of the machinery.

Engines and pumping gear are of special design, and are arranged to control the pumping as occasion requires. The pipes are fitted with relief valves, &c., to save accident.

The details of this plan being of a somewhat complicated nature, we do not propose to enter further into this matter.

Purposes for which hydraulic power can be applied :—Cask raising, lifting malt and hops, coals or yeast, loading out, hauling trucks, working hop and yeast presses, &c.

Cask-raising Machines.—For raising beer from the cellar the most simple is the endless chain lift. Two of these chains, made with long links, work on either side of octagon drums, with stretchers to keep same apart, and having "horns" suitable to the size of the cask required fixed at intervals. The rails are laid with a fall *to* the machine at the bottom, and with a slight fall *from* the machine at the top; by this means it feeds and delivers without labour.

When the cellar is very deep, or it is required to raise casks on to an upper floor, a lift with table working between guides is the most suitable. These can either be worked by steam or hydraulic power—if steam power, either by a special engine on the spot, or from the shafting by cone-barrel gear as before described.

Note.—These machines can be fixed vertical or inclined.

Lowering Casks, &c.—The same kind of machine as above, but consisting only of a table working between guides, with counterbalance gear at back; the top gear consists of a shaft with brake and lever. The casks are rolled on to the table and lowered by gravity, and by means of a spring at the bottom working through a hole in the table, are tipped off on to the rails and roll away; the brake is then released, and the table rises by the counter-balance to the top. No steam power is required. This is the most rapid way to lower casks, and also very economical.

Loading out Beer.—Crane jibs are the most suitable, unless the place will admit of "lifts." These can be worked by special steam hoists, cone barrels, or patent gear, as before described; or where there are a large number required, hydraulic power can be used with much advantage.

Where beer is stacked in cask in the yard, and it is required to load the same in railway trucks, steam portable cranes have been found the most efficient.

Endless Bands are also used to convey grains, malt, &c., to any distance under cover; they are worked by gear from the shafting.

Hop Elevators are made much the same as the ordinary "Jacob," except that the buckets are made of iron, and the chains of steel in lieu of leather bands.

Coal Elevators.—Where coals have to be lifted to a copper fixed on an upper floor, the work can be done—

By Cone-barrel Gear (as before described); the coal is raised in a steel bucket, and tipped out at the top by self-acting gear; if desired, it can be weighed at the same time. Should, however, the coppers be at some distance from the point of "hoisting," it is advisable to raise the coal in small trucks upon a "lift" table or platform, and run the trucks on rails to the desired point.

"**Jacobs**" are also used, much the same as described for the hops, except that the buckets are made like large scoops; they are arranged to discharge into a hopper on upper floor, these are only used in very large places.

Hauling Trucks, &c.—In large breweries, where the railway lines come into the premises, the trucks can be hauled by hydraulic or steam capstans worked by the machinery from the main part of the brewery.

In very large establishments, however, it has been found more economical to use small locomotives.

CHAPTER X.

GRIST CASES AND HOPPERS.

After trying many experiments as to the best material for making grist cases, and with regard to the delivery or the facility with which grist will run over the surface, we have come to the conclusion that there is nothing equal to well-seasoned deal; and in order to render the case perfectly tight, the boards should be ploughed and tongued.

In some situations wrought-iron hoppers are very suitable; the joints should be carefully made, and the whole should be flush riveted on the inside. One of the objections we have found against the use of wrought or cast iron, or similar materials, is that the moisture in the atmosphere at certain seasons condenses on the cold surfaces referred to, when the grist coming in contact gets damp, and hangs about the case.

The usual allowance for hoppers intended for whole grain is 10 cubic feet for every quarter; for grist cases about 12 cubic feet; and in order to avoid "trimming," a little additional space is required. The inclination or angle of the bottoms of hoppers should not be less than 45°, and where self-acting or external mashing machines are adopted, an angle of 50° will be better still, as in such cases it is absolutely necessary, in order to obtain an even mash, that the grist should run very freely. At the lower part of the case it is advisable to have a tickler or disturber to start the grist, especially if a stoppage takes place or it becomes "balled up" from damp or contact with the liquor. This specially applies where Steel's or any other external machine is attached direct to the outlet of the case. The slide at outlet should be fitted with a rack and pinion, or some such mechanism for opening and closing, as the brewer can by such means regulate the supply with much greater precision than when the slide has only to be pulled out. Where there is more than one outlet, all the slides should be so connected that they are acted upon at the same time, so that the grist is delivered in the mash tun equally.

CHAPTER XI.

BOILING.

THIS important process in practical brewing has given rise to endless discussion as to whether wort should be boiled by fire or steam, in open or close coppers, by steam coils or steam jackets. As to the merits of the different systems, we must leave that to the brewers to decide. The system of boiling in a back or copper by a steam coil appears quite to have gone out. With regard to the point of expense in erecting the different systems, there is not much difference between them; in the one case there is the cost of the copper plus setting, against copper plus jacket, plus steam connection. With regard to the working of the plant under the different systems, the *cost of coals* is as nearly equal as possible, whether boiling by fire or by steam. *The size of the copper* should be so calculated that the total contents will be equal to about *one-third* more than the quantity to be boiled.

Hot Liquor Backs.—For heating the water for mashing, in some instances the water is boiled in coppers fitted with "attemperators" to reduce the temperature to the required heat. As a rule, this arrangement is considered unnecessarily elaborate, the general practice being merely to let in a sufficient quantity of cold water to reduce the temperature to the required degree. As a rule, the most convenient arrangement is to have a vessel either of copper or wrought iron (wood is not advisable, as under such circumstances it decays so rapidly), heated by a coil. The best form of coil is the one made of three or four small pipes brazed into one flange, as it gives, in comparison with the area of the pipes, a very much larger heating surface than when the coil is formed of a single pipe; thus a coil formed of four pipes, each 1½ inch in diameter, gives a heating surface of 18 inches, with an area of 7 inches, whereas a coil formed of a single pipe, with a circumference or heating surface of 18 inches, gives an area of steam space equal to 28 inches, thus requiring a much larger amount of steam to do the work.

In several instances we have introduced with good results iron "backs," with double bottoms or steam space, thus doing away with the steam coil. This arrangement allows of the "back" to be the more readily cleaned; but it is not suited, however, to a deep back, as there would not be sufficient heating surface. Heating water by blowing a jet of steam direct into it should never be adopted for brewing water, as there are certain impurities in the boiler, which are sure to get carried over by the steam and mixed with the water, and which must, of course, act prejudicially upon the beer.

If the water has to be heated rapidly, the steam

should merely be blown through the coils or jacket. Where, however, time is of no object, the outlet pipe may either be fitted with a steam trap, so that only the condensed water can get away, or the outlet pipe may be connected to the boiler. In either case the work should be a little stronger, as it would have to resist the working pressure of the boiler.

The following table gives the temperature of steam when working at different pressures, exclusive of the pressure of the atmosphere :—

Lb.	Degrees Fahr.	Lb.	Degrees Fahr.
0	213	60	308
10	240	70	316
20	259	80	324
30	275	90	333
40	288	100	340
50	298	110	344

Hop Backs.—In small breweries these are usually made of "fir," provided with a false bottom. Vent places are formed of plates fixed in one or more corners of the "back."

Copper is, however, in all cases the best material; they are usually made of metal 6 lb. per foot, with an iron band at the outside top edge, over which the copper sheets should be neatly turned. All joints should be flush, and the rivets countersunk. The false bottom can be made of gun metal or copper plates, and either have drilled or slotted holes. When of copper, the holes are cut out by a steel punch ; when of gun metal they are either slotted or drilled with fine holes, being well countersunk below. The slotted plates give the largest area for drainage; the plates should be well fitted at the edges and made perfectly flat.

The back should be well supported at the bottom and should be sufficiently high above the floor to permit of examination of the joints, and also to give space for washing out.

CHAPTER XII.

COOLERS.

WITH many brewers, coolers are now considered unnecessary, and it is contended that exposing the wort so freely to the atmosphere has a damaging effect upon its keeping qualities. Where such opinions are held, it is necessary to have a powerful refrigerator, commanded by a deep receiver or "back," capable of holding the entire "gyle," into which the wort is pumped from the hop-back. Where, however, coolers are adopted, they should be of sufficient capacity to contain the whole "gyle," and arranged for the wort to flow over the first cooler, and back over a second. This arrangement allows the wort to travel some little distance before reaching the refrigerator. The material of which coolers are constructed varies according to the views held by the brewers; where iron is not objected to, it is one of the best materials to be used, being cheap, and easily cleaned; if iron be used, the plates of which the cooler is composed should be cast moderately thin, and arrangements should be made for a free current of air beneath them; cooling will then go on both from above and beneath. The hot wort should not be delivered on the coolers at one particular spot, but allowed to flow on from a wood trough, the whole width of the first cooler; the metal will then expand regularly under the action of the heat, and so save fracture; whereas, if the wort is delivered in one corner, the plates immediately surrounding are liable to crack, especially in frosty weather; it should not be made wide for the same reason. Where expense is not objected to, the best coolers by far are those constructed of copper; great care is required in putting them together to keep the plates quite flat, so as to allow of proper drainage. Coolers have been constructed of glazed tiles on brick arches; this, however, is a bad plan. On account of there being so many joints, it is next to impossible to keep them sweet; and, from being so thick, the heat is retained, and for a long "gyle" rather tends to impart than subtract heat; the expense, moreover, in the first instance, is also great. If wood coolers are erected, the boards should be in narrow widths, and be equal in length to the width of the cooler; no heading joints should be allowed, as it is impossible to keep a cooler tight under such circumstances.

Fans are occasionally fixed where there is not sufficient current of air; it is advisable to fix at least two in the length of each cooler to distribute the air more equally.

CHAPTER XIII.

REFRIGERATORS AND ICE MACHINES.

Refrigerators.—The points to be considered in the selection of a refrigerator are: first, the simplicity of its construction; second, the facility with which every part can be cleaned; and third, the economy of its working, in regard to the quantity of water required to cool down a given quantity of wort. There is a considerable difference of opinion amongst brewers as to whether wort is injured by being minutely subdivided, as in some of the upright refrigerators, where the wort is allowed to fall in drops upon the cooling pipes. Where this is not considered objectionable, and there is sufficient height between the coolers or receiver and the tuns, the upright refrigerators, as a rule give the most satisfaction, and this from the circumstance that not only can the surfaces be readily cleaned, but also the water-ways. This last is a matter of considerable importance, as the matter deposited from the water, being a bad conductor of heat, if the pipes are allowed to fur up, the water cannot exert its full cooling power upon the wort. There are so many varieties of flat refrigerators, that to name any one in particular here would only be to mislead the mind of the reader, as the kind to be adopted depends somewhat upon the conditions under which it is to be worked. It may, however, be taken as a general rule that the wort-ways should be exposed to view, as cleanliness is so absolutely necessary in brewing. Again, the simpler a refrigerator is in construction the better, as where there are many joints—from the continual expansion and contraction going on—leakages, sooner or later, are sure to ensue. The most satisfactory in working are those in which the wort is kept constantly moving by a slight motion of the liquor-ways or pipes. As far as possible, all refrigerators in a wooden case or "back" should be avoided.

Where liquor that has been through a cooling machine is used for refrigerating, the most economical arrangement is either to have two refrigerators coupled together, using ordinary liquor in the first, and the cooled liquor in the second, or to have the refrigerator constructed so that for two-thirds of the tubes "ordinary," and for the remaining portion the cooled liquor can be used.

Ice and Cooling Machines.—No brewery of any size should be without an ice-making machine, not necessarily for making ice, but for cooling water, it being more convenient generally to have a supply of cold water at 40° or 45° temperature for refrigerating and attemperating purposes than a supply of ice.

There are several different descriptions of machines now at work; the general principle of all is the same, viz. the evaporation of a volatile liquid in vacuo, the liquid used being either ether, bisulphide of carbon, acetone, or ammonia. For cooling water with a machine in which ether is employed, the water to be cooled passes through the tubes of a refrigerator, such tubes being inserted in an air-tight case. The ether which is contained in the refrigerator is evaporated by means of a vacuum pump abstracting the heat from the water passing through the refrigerator.

The ether, now in the form of vapour, passes into a condenser, where, under a slight pressure by the aid of a stream of water, it is again reduced to its liquid form and can be worked over again; thus the same ether can be used continuously without any appreciable loss. Another form of machine in which ammonia is employed, cold is produced by direct action, without the intervention of mechanical power. The process may be briefly described as follows:—A strong solution of ammonia is pumped into the top of an analyzing column, similar to those used in continuous distillation of spirit; the solution in falling meets an ascending current of steam, thus eliminating the ammonia from the water; then, passing through a refrigerator, it is deprived of all water, and afterwards is liquefied by its own pressure. The liquefied ammonia passes to the cooling cylinder, in which is a coil of pipe, through which the liquid to be cooled is allowed to flow, and then, resuming its aërified condition, abstracts the heat from the liquid to be acted upon. Passing into a vessel called the absorber, it meets the exhaust liquor of the distilling apparatus, and being dissolved in it, forms the solution of ammonia with which we started.

Another distinct class of cold-producing machines, more suitable for cooling air for tun-rooms, cellars, &c., are those working with compressed air—that is, the air is compressed by means of an air pump and cooled whilst in a state of compression by means of a jet of water, and then allowed to expand, the degree of temperature being regulated by the amount of compression. With a machine working on this principle we have known a fermenting tun-room in a German brewery maintained at a temperature of 34° F.; but as far as the data could be obtained, this class of machine is not so economically worked as either an ether or ammonia machine.

Where a large supply of ice is required in summer, it is sometimes an advantage to erect an ice-house for storing rough ice, the least expensive form of which is to construct it entirely of timber boarding on the inside and outside of the framing, and filling the interstice with sawdust, thatching the roof, care being taken to provide good drainage, as damp is as much to be feared as heat.

CHAPTER XIV.

FERMENTING TUNS.

The construction of the tuns depends upon the system of brewing adopted. For example, if the Yorkshire plan is pursued, the tuns or fermenting vessels must be constructed of stone slabs; but under ordinary circumstances the vessels are best made of yellow (not white) Dantzic planks, as free as possible from all shakes, sap, or knots. Where space is an object, they should be constructed square; if skimming is practised, this form is most convenient; but where there is plenty of room, round vessels have the advantage, as they are more easily cleaned, and are much more easily kept in repair, as in the event of any leakage it can nearly always be stopped by driving the hoops. The most perfect tuns, no doubt, are those made of slate, and although of course more expensive to erect in the first instance, yet in the end they are decidedly more economical. The objection often raised to tuns of this description is, that slate being a much better conductor of heat than wood, any change of temperature is the more readily communicated to the contents. That this is no real or serious objection, is proved by the success with which brewing is carried on where they have been adopted. The practice of fitting heads to fermenting tuns appears to have nearly gone out. Where circular wood tuns are employed, the simplest and best way is to allow the staves to run up, so as to form the yeast boarding, having a manhole cut in front fitted with sliding doors. And in square tuns, although the expense may be a trifle more, by far the best plan is to construct the tuns of sufficient depth, allowing for the yeast, having a manhole cut in front as before mentioned. By this arrangement, the tuns are much more easily cleaned, as there are no corners or angles for the dirt to collect in. Where the yeast boarding is constructed of a lighter substance than the rest of the tun, the bottom board round the whole of the tun should be so fitted as to be easily removed when washing out the tun. No tun is complete without a powerful "attemperator," supplied with hot and cold water. For large tuns, the simplest form is to have three or four coils of tinned copper pipe fixed to the sides of the tuns by wood or gun-metal brackets. But for smaller tuns it is generally found convenient to have movable "attemperators" hung with chains and balance weights, and connected with the water mains by indiarubber hose. When brewing upon the Yorkshire system, the fermenting tuns are constructed of stone slabs with heads fixed some little way down in the tun, dividing it into two parts; a hole being cut in the head, the yeast is thrown up into the upper part of the tun. There have been various patents taken out for fitting adjusting-heads to tuns, so as to lower the heads to the level of the wort, allowing the yeast to work out through "swan necks," so combining the fermenting tun and union casks. For brewing porter or stout, the tuns may be of any size, containing in some instances, in some of the London breweries, from 1500 to 1800 barrels. For ale, however, the size of the tun should be limited, from 60 to 120 barrels being a good size.

Skimming is usually done by hand. When the tuns are round, a very useful machine is one consisting of centre shaft and adjustable revolving skimmer; when it is required to "skim," the board is set to the necessary height, and the yeast swept down the parachute, which is suspended in the usual way.

CHAPTER XV.

CLEANSING VESSELS.

In many establishments the old system of cleansing in casks resting on "stillions" is still in use; the yeast finding its way as it can into the stillion beneath. A slight improvement is occasionally introduced, viz. having a light movable copper shoot fitted to the bung-hole of the casks, so as to direct the yeast into the stillion. The "topping-up" being done by hand, involves a great deal of hand labour. For porter or stout, slate vessels are much preferable to any other description, and where adopted, the readiest way is to have the space devoted to the erection of the vessels paved or floored with slate slabs; upon this floor the sides of the vessels are fixed, dividing the space into the requisite number of troughs. By this arrangement, the intermediate spaces serve for yeast stillions; thus No. 1, 3, 4, 6, 7, &c., would contain the beer, while 2, 5, &c., would serve for yeast stillions. It is generally advisable to subdivide these troughs by transverse divisions, allowing each division to hold from six to fifteen barrels, according to the trade done. In most cases, these divisions are closed in with slate heads, with a manhole, for the yeast to work out. To complete the arrangement, each set should have a self-acting apparatus for "topping-up," the simplest form for which is to have a small receiver fitted at such a level as to command the cleansing vessels, in which is arranged a valve attached to a lever, which lever is acted upon by a copper float, so that as the level of the beer falls, the valve opens and admits a sufficient quantity to pass into the vessels from the parachute, so as to maintain the level at the required height. In place of having "attemperators" fixed to each division, the temperature can be regulated by allowing warm or cold water to flow over the tops or heads of the vessels.

No brewing question perhaps has been so keenly discussed as the advantages or disadvantages of the "Burton Union" system, and it certainly is a very doubtful point whether it is advisable for a brewer, doing a small trade, to adopt it. One of the most important points to be attended to is the keeping of the various utensils scrupulously clean; and there is no denying that the "Union" casks, with the connection, and especially if fitted with "attemperators," which now has become the universal practice at Burton, do require a very great deal of care in washing out; and unless the men are closely looked after, the casks do not get that amount of attention necessary for ensuring success in brewing a uniformly good article.

The casks are usually made to contain from 90 to 160 gallons each; in some instances the charging main is connected by means of a union to the trunnion of the cask, the trunnion being cast hollow, so as to allow of the cask revolving for cleaning without having to disconnect the main; but this plan is not desirable, as there is a difficulty in keeping the joint tight, and the joint forms a harbour for dirt. There should be at least two sample taps in each set, and every cask should be fitted with an attemperator; many different patterns are used, but upon no consideration should any be introduced that cannot be readily removed and replaced when and after washing out. The yeast troughs should also be fitted with attemperators.

Framing for carrying Union casks should be supported on cast-iron standards, and the mains carried on cast-iron brackets.

Troughs.—The feeding and yeast troughs are sometimes made of wood, but are best made of slate.

In many instances, in porter and stout breweries, the beer is cleansed in open iron troughs, the end of each trough being divided off to form a receptacle for the yeast after it is skimmed off.

Vats.—The practice of vatting beer has almost been discontinued. Where, however, vats are to be erected, they should, of course, be of oak—English oak is the most durable. The vats should be situated in a place where the temperature can be maintained at a moderately low and regular degree all the year round; they are also best placed on iron columns and framing, both on account of utilizing the space below, and also because the electrical currents, which are continually traversing the earth, have an injurious effect upon beer stored in vessels sunk in the ground. Deep vats having a small area are generally to be preferred to those of lesser depth and larger area. It was formerly thought that it was advantageous to erect the vats with the larger diameter at the top. This idea, however, is now completely exploded, and they are erected with the smaller diameter at the top.

CHAPTER XVI.

PIPES.

All wort "mains" should be of tinned copper pipe, in moderate lengths, with unions, allowing for disconnection and cleaning. They should be laid to a fall of not less than 1 inch in 10 feet for draining, and those pipes which cannot drain themselves, such as "stand pipes" from pumps, &c., should be fitted with small draining cocks.

All the cocks and valves should be of gun metal, and if any sluice valves are inserted in the "wort mains" they should have gun-metal valves and cases. It is also a great advantage to have the various cocks fitted with a dial, to show plainly when open or shut.

All waste pipes from the utensils should not upon any account be connected directly to the drain, but should first deliver into an open cistern, because in the event of any waste valve being left open, there is a chance of it being detected at once, with possibly the loss of a barrel or less, instead of the whole "gyle."

For the water and steam pipes, either wrought or cast iron answers the purpose, according to the size. Where cast-iron pipes are used, they should be connected with faced flanges, drilled holes, and bolts, and nuts; all bends either in the copper or iron pipes should be as easy as possible, and all sharp elbows most carefully avoided. Air cocks should be fixed at bends to let out the air. If the steam pipes are of any length, an expansion joint should be inserted so as to allow of the pipes expanding and contracting without straining the joints; the best form of expansion joint being a U bend, made of copper or copper disc, as then no packed joint is required, and a continual source of annoyance avoided. A cock should always be inserted in all water mains as close as possible to the tank from which the supply is drawn, so as to be able to shut off the water and drain the mains in frosty weather. The flanges of all steam pipes should be faced, and the joints made with red lead.

Lead pipe lined with pure tin is now manufactured, which effectually protects the lead from any corrosive action of the water; and Dr. Schwarz, of Breslau, notes a simple method of protecting lead pipes from the action of water by forming on the inside surface of the pipes an insoluble sulphide of lead. The operation, which is a very simple one, consists in filling the pipes with a warm and concentrated solution of sulphide of potassium or sodium; the solution is left in contact with the lead for about fifteen minutes.

For calculating the delivery of water through pipes, the following is the formula :—

$$W = \cdot 8 \frac{\sqrt{D^5}}{\sqrt{\frac{L}{H}}}.$$

W = barrels delivered per minute.
D = diameter in inches.
L = length of main } in feet.
H = head }

And the following formula gives the diameter of a pipe necessary to pass a given quantity :—

$$D = 1 \cdot 1 \sqrt[5]{\frac{L \times W^2}{H}}.$$

NOTE.—The square, cube, fourth, and fifth powers of a few useful numbers will be found in the tables at the end of this work.

As an example :—How many barrels per minute would pass through a 4-inch main, 200 feet long, 50 feet head? Then by the first formula

$$W = \cdot 8 \frac{\sqrt{4^5}}{\sqrt{\frac{200}{50}}} = \cdot 8 \frac{\sqrt{1024}}{\sqrt{4}} = \cdot 8 \frac{32}{2} \text{ or } 16 \times \cdot 8 = 12 \cdot 8 \text{ brls.}$$

Second example :—What should be the diameter of a main to pass twelve barrels per minute, through a 200-foot main, having a head of 50 feet? Then from the second formula

$$D = 1 \cdot 1 \sqrt[5]{\frac{200 \times 144}{50}} = 1 \cdot 1 \sqrt[5]{576} = 3 \cdot 5 \times 1 \cdot 1$$

$= 3 \cdot 85$ inches as requisite diameter of main.

And for estimating the pressure in pounds per square inch due to the head of liquor, multiply the height of the column in feet by 0·434.

Example: the pressure in pounds per square inch at the lowest end of a main 100 feet high would be

$$100 \times \cdot 434 = 43 \cdot 4 \text{ lb. per square inch.}$$

CHAPTER XVII.

HOP AND YEAST PRESSES.

During the last few years there have been many different kinds of hop presses introduced. For a small plant there are several very compact presses in which the pressure is obtained in the old way with a screw, or the screw in combination with gearing, the presses being worked either by hand or steam power. In selecting a press, particular attention should be paid to the removal of the pressed hops, as in some of the more recent ones the cylinder or box in which the hops are pressed can be drawn up clear of the hops, thus admitting of the hops being removed in a solid mass. The most complete presses for larger establishments are those worked by hydraulic power, as they do their work rapidly and most effectually; the amount of pressure which can be brought to bear upon the hops is only limited by the strength of the machine.

But whatever description of press is selected, either for hops or "drawings," the chief point to keep in view is the ease with which they can be thoroughly cleaned.

Hop Presses, Hydraulic Power.—The hops are placed in a box with a perforated lining of copper, having a space all round to take the "drawings." The bottom of the box is made loose; when the "ram" head rises, this loose bottom carries up the hops and presses them against a fixed piston or ram at the top of the press. Two boxes are usually supplied, to run in and out on rails either fixed in the floor or near the head of the press; in this case they are more easily filled and the pressed cake discharged, one box being filled while the other is being pressed, thus a large quantity can be done at one time.

Another arrangement is to have the cylinder in which the hops are pressed, fixed; after pressing, the cover is opened, and the ram clears the pressed hops, so that they may be removed in block.

Screw Presses.—For ordinary breweries, a screw press, of which there are many varieties, is usually fixed in the hop back. The "pressings" can be pumped up by the usual wort pumps.

Steam power is generally applied from the nearest shafting, thus saving hand labour.

Yeast Presses.—The best kind of presses are those in which the yeast is pumped into bags fixed between intermediate plates secured in position by a screw. The yeast comes out in dry cakes. The machines are made to take apart readily for the purpose of cleaning.

Those made in iron are the most desirable, they are more easily cleaned and not so likely to get foul.

The pumping apparatus is usually attached to the machine, but in large places the pumps are worked by special engine or from the shafting.

CHAPTER XVIII.

COOPERAGE.

An important question is being continually asked, viz. What is the best method of cleansing and purifying brewers' casks? With regard to cleansing, there have been many machines brought out since the first one was patented in 1843, but the original pattern machine is still in use in many establishments, although many better machines have been introduced. But for thoroughly cleansing a cask, one of the best, if not the best, was patented some few years since, and known as the "screw disc cask machine." This machine is particularly suited to large firms, as it is made capable of holding and cleaning from three to fourteen casks at one time, and of cleaning 250 casks per day. The operation is as follows: In each foul cask is placed a small portion of shingle and a quantity of hot water; the cask is then placed in the machine, and after from ten to twenty minutes' working, all the surface impurities will have been removed. The casks have to be sluiced out, and are then perfectly clean; the cost of the entire operation not exceeding 5*s.* per hundred casks. For purifying stinking or sour casks, they are charged with hot liquor and the liquor boiled in the casks for a considerable time by a supply of steam. It cannot be too well known that there is nothing so destructive to casks as excessive steaming; and for this reason, steam is the most powerful solvent, and every time a cask is steamed to any extent, the gums which nature has provided for binding the fibres of the wood together are dissolved, and a fresh series of fibres are laid bare and exposed. Thus denuded of the natural residue of the sap, and exposed to the action of air and water, and minute vesicles of air entangled in the fibre, there is induced a great tendency in the timber to another decay. The system known as the hot-air process is now not only in use throughout Burton, Dublin, &c., but by many of the leading establishments throughout the kingdom. The process is as follows: The casks are slightly steamed, and then a current of hot air is impelled into them at a temperature of 350° of heat, when all taint will be removed (with the exception of about one cask in 200), and the germs of all mouldiness killed. The system has been violently attacked by various persons, as it was asserted that exposing the casks to such a high temperature must necessarily destroy the wood, rendering it brittle, &c.; but practice has utterly confuted all such theory, it having been proved by those who have used it the largest, that the wood is rendered more dense and the casks more staunch under the hot-air process. The objection has arisen from not understanding the difference in action between heat in a quiescent state, and when impelled at a great velocity; for if wood is dried in an oven heated to 350° the timber will be brittle, the gums being to a certain extent destroyed; if, however, the timber is placed in a current of air heated to the same degree, the water or moisture *only* will be evaporated. Or to illustrate the difference in another way. If a piece of meat is placed in the oven we all know the result; whereas if the same piece had been exposed to a current of air at the same temperature, the meat would have been *dried* and not *cooked*. There are many advantages to be derived from using the hot-air system, as besides purifying the casks, they are rendered perfectly dry, and the result is that the beers are preserved in much better condition. In one establishment it was found that the same "gyle," after being racked off when drawn from the different casks, varied much in condition and flavour; the hot-air process was, however, adopted, and such variations in quality ceased to occur, the casks having all been rendered uniformly dry before filling. A moment's consideration will show how important it must be to have a cask thoroughly dry, for if beer is put into a damp bottle, or drawn in a damp jug, the beer becomes flat directly. How prejudicial then it must be to put beer into a cask which contains from 1 to 3 lb. of water in the staves. Considering then that the hot-air apparatus is the most expeditious and effectual process for purifying casks, that they are improved by it, and the apparatus soon pays for itself in causing fewer leakages and fewer returns, it follows as a natural consequence that no establishment should be without one.

In the arrangement of a cooperage, regard should be had to the delivery of the dirty casks and the position of the stores, so that there should not be any unnecessary labour in rolling them about. As a general rule, for a repairing shop the width should not be less than 20 feet, and the blocks not less than 7 feet apart; provision should be made for "firing" the casks; it is also necessary to provide store room for hoops, flags, &c., which should be in a loft over the shop. The old staves and ends cut up into 4-inch lengths, and set in concrete, make a first-rate floor for a cooperage; by each block should be fixed an iron plate for placing the casks when driving the hoops.

Machinery has been introduced to a certain extent for cask-making; but with the exception of one or two of the simpler machines, such as for sawing or hoop-bending, it does not pay a brewer to use it. The only firms who can work a machine cooperage to advantage are those who go in for large export orders, when a number of casks are wanted at a short notice, the time taken to turn out a barrel being much less than if made by hand. In a machine cooperage we once visited, from the moment the staves were taken off the stack until the cask was complete was thirty-five minutes; but as the size of the plant to be of use must be equal to an emergency, it follows that the greater part remains idle a large portion of the year, and the interest on capital, repairs, and power required for driving amount to as much, or nearly as much, as the saving effected in wages.

CHAPTER XIX.

MALTINGS.

Except in some matters of detail, the arrangement of an English malt-house has remained unchanged for many years, due no doubt in a great measure to the Excise laws. Speaking generally, a malting should be designed with the cistern and couch at one end of the floors, and the kiln at the opposite end; the malt store either on the floor over the working floors, or in a building attached to the kiln, in which case the ground floor of the store should be left for screening and sacking up. The barley chambers, screening rooms, and bins should be over the cistern. The size of the house and site will determine the number of working floors—either one, two, or three.

The Cistern.—The cistern can be constructed either of iron or brick; if of ordinary brick, it should be built in cement, finished inside with a coating of Portland cement; but the best bricks to use are the white glazed bricks set in cement. The cistern will require a drain down the centre covered with perforated plates. According to the Excise laws, the cistern must be constructed so that the sides and ends are at right angles; the bottom may have a slight fall towards the drain in the centre; the depth must not exceed 40 inches, nor the width 8 feet, and there must be a clear space of 48 inches over every part of the cistern, in order that the Excise officer may take the gauge, and there must be a good light. If there are two working floors in a house, the cistern may be placed midway between the floors, so that the grain may be thrown up or down, and save the labour of hoisting any portion; and for three floors the cistern can be placed between the upper and middle floor. On the other hand, it saves expense in constructing a house to keep the cistern on the ground floor, and hoist to the upper floors. The allowance for size of cistern is 12¼ cubic feet per quarter; it is, however, an advantage to allow rather more than that quantity, as then in the cold weather it permits of an extra quantity being "steeped." The most approved method of supplying the cistern with water is by means of a perforated pipe running the whole length.

The Couch.—The couch should be calculated to allow of at least 13½ cubic feet per quarter, but for the same reason as before it will be as well to allow a rather greater capacity. According to the Excise laws the ends and one side must be permanent; all the angles right angles; the depth must not exceed 30 inches; the front to be constructed of boards not less than 2 inches thick, firmly secured to uprights.

Working Floors.—The area of floor allowed per quarter varies very considerably in England; the dimensions we have taken at different houses range from 110 superficial feet per quarter up to 190 feet. For making best malt, if the house is to be worked up to its full capacity at the beginning and end of the season, 170 to 180 feet per quarter should be allowed, but in general the floors are of a less area than that, working up above the average during the cold season, when the floors can be worked thicker, and reducing the quantity during the warmer weather. The breadth should not be more than 40 to 50 feet; if the floors exceed these dimensions there is sometimes a difficulty in regulating the temperature.

Many experiments have been made as to the best material for constructing floors, but at present nearly all are finished with either cement or tiles. In the Burton-on-Trent and Newark districts, tiles are almost universally adopted. Great care should be taken in selecting a tile of a uniform make and density, and also particular care should be taken in the setting, in order to ensure a uniform and perfectly level floor; if the tiles are not perfectly true the corn gets damaged and bruised when being turned. Portland cement makes a very good floor, and can be used either on boards or as concrete between rolled-iron joists for the upper floors. The height of a floor should just give head room, say 6 feet 6 inches in the clear of all timbers or girders.

The window openings should be fitted with shutters, and should be made to slide, and not hung with hinges. Opinions differ as to whether the openings should be fitted with glass; but, on the whole, it appears desirable, as the temperature can be better regulated than when shutters only are provided.

It is a very great advantage for the floors to be uniform in width, and straight; that is, as far as possible, the floors should form a rectangular parallelogram.

Kilns.—The malt kilns, as before stated, should be placed at the end of the working floor. Various plans have been introduced, from time to time, for constructing the floors, such as punched iron plates, wove wire, haircloth, &c., but by far the greater number of floors are now laid with tiles, and the manufacture of these tiles, by certain firms, has now reached a great state of perfection—the holes, 1200 to a square foot, are cut through exceedingly clean, no "burr" being left to check the free current of air. The tiles should be selected of a uniform thickness and of a perfectly level surface. Wire floors, if well laid, will last many years and will offer much less resistance to the air, as they give about 6900 holes to the square foot. The usual allowance is from 20 feet to 25 feet super. for pale malt—the height of the kiln floor above the firing floor being from 16 to 25 feet. According to description of malt to be dried, the arrangement of the firing must depend upon the opinion of the maltster—some preferring to have the firing place fixed with ordinary furnace bars, &c., whilst others consider it best to have the fires in movable furnaces.

Many kilns have been constructed with merely an open ventilator running down the ridge of roof, or at the apex of roof of the square kiln; and, although the malt can be thoroughly dried on such kilns, nevertheless it is at an increased expenditure of fuel; and it has been demonstrated over and over again, that for regular and economical drying, a cowl is by far the best in a malting. In one altered under our direction some short time since, a cowl was substituted for a fixed ventilator—the result being a more regular drying of the malt in a shorter time, and with less consumption of fuel.

Kilns have been erected in which mechanical means have been employed, such as forcing a large volume of air by means of a fan through the malt, the air having been heated by passing over a steam-heated surface, the temperature being regulated by means of a cold air inlet with a regulating valve—the object being to ensure perfect drying at a low temperature. Whether malt so dried is of equally good flavour as when dried in the ordinary way over open fires, is a question for the maltster to decide.

Foreign Maltings.—The ordinary type of a German or Belgian malting is a house with a cistern, no couch, one or two working floors, and a kiln with two drying floors and a firing place arranged according to the plan given (Plate XX.), a large number being fitted with Schlemmer's apparatus for turning the malt on the drying floors. In most of the large establishments the working floors are constructed below the ground level, whereby a more regular temperature can be maintained.

Pneumatic Malting.—Considerable attention has been directed lately to the subject of Pneumatic Malting; the system was first patented by Mr. Tizard, in the year 1852, the principle being to keep a current of cold and moist air moving through the grain when germinating. The general arrangement of a malting on this system would be an ordinary cistern and couch; but afterwards, instead of throwing the grain on to the usual working floors, it would be thrown from the couch into a second vessel about 3 feet deep, fitted with a perforated false bottom, an exhaust fan would be connected to the space below this false bottom, and a current of air, previously cooled and rendered moist (which can be effected in several ways), is drawn through the grain during the germination. The mass will require turning about every twelve hours; when ready the malt would be dried on an ordinary kiln. The advantages claimed for this process of malting are complete control over the germination, as the temperature of the air can be regulated to any required degree, whereby a perfectly sound malt may be produced; the power of working through the summer months; less labour is required; and a great saving of floor space.

Another system which has been making some progress is that known as "Gecmen's" system, and may be called a mechanical malting. The apparatus consists of a series of floors, about twenty-five in number, and 10 to 12 inches apart, each floor being 17 ft. by 8 ft. wide, of twenty plates each mounted on spindles, and connected by small cranks to a bar, so that the whole of the plates composing a floor can be turned over simultaneously. The process as carried out is as follows:—After steeping, the top floor is charged, and at the proper time by turning the plates the charge is dropped on to the second floor, and so on until by the time it reaches the lower floor it is ready for the kiln. The temperature can be regulated by means of a fan. From one at work the temperature was 54° on the top floor, from 60° to 65° on the middle floor, and decreased to 54° at the bottom. The advantages claimed for this system are considerable saving of time, labour, expense, avoidance of loss of grain, and as the temperature can be regulated, malting can be carried on through the summer months. A similar apparatus can be used for the kiln, only the plates are perforated and only sixteen floors high, the temperature at the bottom or outlet being from 160° and upwards, according to the quality of the malt produced, the temperature of the top floor being 90°.

There are various other mechanical systems in work, but of all this class of maltings the before-named are the most in use.

CHAPTER XX.

COST OF ERECTION.

THE following estimates have been based upon work carried out to our drawings and under our superintendence; they must, however, be considered *approximate* only, as the cost much depends upon the site and convenience for the delivery of materials, &c.

Again, the cost will be considerably increased unless the whole of the work, that is, buildings and plant, are designed and carried out under one architect and engineer. In all large breweries we prefer to obtain separate estimates for the building, boilers, coppers, millwright's work, and iron utensils, slatework, back work, &c. By such an arrangement the proprietor can deal direct with each manufacturer, without having to pay a second profit.

We have illustrated a few only of the breweries we have erected, giving a general idea of the arrangement to suit various sizes and requirements.

COST OF 5-QUARTER BREWERY. (Plate I.)

Plant, consisting of cast-iron cold liquor back, hot liquor back, malt rolls with hopper and screen, grist case, self-acting mashing machine, mash tun, sparger and false bottom, steam wort copper, hop back, wood cooler, refrigerator, and wood fermenting tuns, racking back, cleansing cask and stillion, set of well pumps and gear, boiler and engine. Well not more than 30 feet deep, including the buildings, say **£2400**

Cost of 7-Quarter Brewery. (Plate II.)

Cornish boiler, engine, shafting and gear, pumps, cold and hot liquor backs, malt hopper, rolls, screen, elevator, grist case, mashing machine, mash tun with sparger, &c., underback, steam copper, hop back, cooler, refrigerator, slate tuns, settling backs, hoist for malt and hops, grain stage, &c. (it will be noticed extensive cellarage is provided, and some portion of the brewery is below ground line; this, of course, *somewhat increases the cost*), including buildings **4500**

Cost of 10-Quarter Brewery. (Plate III.)

Cornish boiler, engine, shafting and gear. Well not exceeding 30 feet, and pumps, cold liquor back, hot liquor back, malt rolls, screen and grist case, Willison's mashing machine, two mash tuns with spargers and false bottoms, copper (fire), hop back, coolers, refrigerator, fermenting tuns with attemperators, cleansing casks, and all pipes and cocks, including buildings **3650**

Cost of 15-Quarter Brewery. (Plate IV.)

Engine and boiler, shafting, &c., cold liquor back, hot liquor copper, malt hopper, screen, rolls, grist case, mashing machine, mash tun, &c., underback, steam wort copper, hop back, cooler, refrigerator, fermenting tuns, malt hoist, &c. *Plant (only) about* **£1800**

COST OF 16-QUARTER BREWERY. (Plate V.)

Boiler, engine, shafting and gear. Well and pumps, cold and hot liquor backs, malt rolls and screen, malt hopper and grist case, mashing machine, mash tuns, &c., underback, two fire coppers, hop back, cooler, refrigerator, fermenting tuns, unions, racking backs, malt hoist, &c., including buildings... ... ... **5300**

COST OF 20-QUARTER BREWERY. (Plate VI.)

Engine and boiler, shafting and gear, cold and hot liquor backs, malt rolls, screen, grist case, malt hopper, Steel's mashing machine, two mash tuns, underback, two fire coppers, hop back, cooler, refrigerator, fermenting tuns, &c., hop and malt stores, including buildings **5400**

COST OF 24-QUARTER BREWERY. (Plate VII.)

Cold and hot liquor backs, malt screw, rolls and hopper, grist case, mashing machine, mash tuns, &c., steam coppers, hop back, coolers, refrigerator, fermenting tuns, hop store, engine and boiler, all shafting and gear, pipes, cocks, attemperators, including buildings **7080**

COST OF 40-QUARTER BREWERY. (Plates VIII. and IX.)

Engine and boiler, shafting, &c., cold and hot liquor backs and liquor copper, malt hopper, rolls, and screen, elevator, grist case, Steel's mashing machine, mash tuns, &c., underback and top back, fire coppers, hop back, coolers, refrigerator, fermenting tuns, racking backs, two steam hoists, hop and malt stores, including buildings **£9500**

COST OF 40-QUARTER BREWERY. (Plates X. and XI.)

Cold and hot liquor backs, malt hopper, rolls, screen and screw, grist case, Willison's mashing machine, two mash tuns, underback with steam coil, fire coppers, hop back, coolers, refrigerators, fermenting tuns, union casks, hoisting apparatus, two sets of pumps, boilers, engines, all gear and shafting, pipes and cocks, including building, about **8950**

COST OF 70-QUARTER BREWERY. (Plates XII. and XIII.)

Cold and hot liquor backs, malt screw, hopper, malt rolls and screen, elevator, grist cases, Steel's mashing machine, mash tuns, fire coppers, hop back, coolers, refrigerator, fermenting tuns, union casks with yeast batches, copper pipes, &c., and racking rounds, engine and boilers, shafting and gear, two sets of pumps and Well, including buildings **20,150**

COST OF 160-QUARTER BREWERY. (Plates XIV. and XV.)

Engines and boilers, shafting and gear, malt hopper, measuring machine, malt rolls and screen, grist cases, cold and hot liquor backs, Steel's mashing machines, mash tuns with gun-metal internal mashing machines, gun-metal false bottoms, underback, fire coppers, hop back of copper, coolers of copper, refrigerators, fermenting tuns, unions, racking rounds, malt bins, screw and elevator, cask hoist, sack tackle for malt and hops, cellars, pipes, cocks, &c., including buildings, about £68,000

COST OF 100-QUARTER MALTING. (Plates XVIII. and XIX.)

The building is constructed with the cistern and couch at one end, with three germinating (or working) floors, with barley store over. At the other end is the kiln, with coke and malt stores, screening rooms, and malt bins and malt stores. These are conveniently placed for loading out into railway trucks on the siding. Cost of building and plant ... 7100

CHAPTER XXI.

DESCRIPTION OF PLATES.

It has been considered advisable to leave out some of the details, as stairs, shafting and gear, and all minor matters, to save complication in the drawings, which are necessarily made to a small scale.

5-Quarter Brewery. (Plate I.)

The cold liquor back is placed to command every utensil in the brewery. Hot liquor back is heated by steam coil. Malt is hoisted by steam tackle, and tipped into the hopper, from which it passes over the screen, and through the rolls, to grist case. From the mash tun the worts run direct into the copper, which is heated by steam by means of an iron jacket; it then passes to the hop back over the coolers to the refrigerator, then to the fermenting tuns, and lastly to cleansing casks (or racking back). The boiler is placed in a separate building, and the engine near same, thus the temperature of the tun room is not affected. Brewer's room can either be on the mash tun stage or in tun room. This brewery was designed to work with a malting; as the buildings are reduced to the smallest limits there is very little room to store malt and hops in the brewery.

7-Quarter Brewery. (Plate II.)

Cold and hot liquor backs fixed as before, the latter heated by steam coil.

Malt is raised by the steam hoist to the store and tipped into the hopper, runs over the screen through rolls, is then carried up by the elevator to the grist case to mash tun fitted with sparger and mashing machine. The wort is run off into underback, then to the steam copper, passing afterwards to hop back over the coolers to the refrigerators; it then goes to the slate tuns and settling backs.

The brewer's room is placed on the mash-tun stage. The boiler is in a separate building. It will be observed very extensive cellarage is provided, and a good part of the brewery sunk below the ground line; this plan, while possessing many advantages, increases the cost of the building, though in many respects it much facilitates the working.

Loading stage is about level with the drays; the casks are raised from the cellars by steam power.

10-Quarter Brewery. (Plate III.)

Cold liquor back is erected at top, and hot liquor back under, this is heated with steam coil. Malt is brought up by steam tackle to the malt hopper, and passes over the screen through the rolls to grist case, which is fitted with Willison's mashing machine, and commands the two mash tuns; the wort then passes to the fire copper, which is fixed to command the hop back, and then pumped up to the coolers fixed above, from these it runs through refrigerators to fermenting tuns and cleansing casks. The boiler and copper are situated in a separate building, the engine under the mash tuns. The loading stage is about level with the drays; if desired, the casks can be raised from the cellar to this level by steam power, and could then be rolled on the drays with very little labour.

15-Quarter Brewery. (Plate IV.)

Cast-iron liquor back is on the top of the building. Hot liquor copper fixed near the wort copper. Malt is pulled up by steam tackle, and passes over screen to malt rolls and grist case. Steel's machine fixed to the outlet, mash tun with mashing machine; wort runs out into underback, and pumped up to the steam wort copper, then runs into hop back over the cooler and through refrigerator to fermenting tuns and racking room. Engine and boiler are in a separate building.

16-Quarter Brewery. (Plate V.)

Cold and hot liquor backs are fixed, as before; malt is pulled up by steam tackle, and passes over the screen through the rolls to grist case; there are two mash tuns with spargers and mashing machines; the wort is let out into the underback, and then to the fire coppers, which with the boiler and hop back are fixed in a separate building. From the hop back it is pumped up to the coolers, passes through the refrigerator to the tuns and "unions," then to the racking backs and loading stage or cellars. The engine is fixed under the mash tuns. The brewer's room is on the mash-tun stage. There is a grain stage to facilitate the delivery to the carts.

20-Quarter Brewery. (Plate VI.)

Cold and hot liquor backs are fixed at top of brewery; malt, after being ground, is taken up by the elevator to the grist case, to which is fixed a Steel's machine to serve the two tuns; the wort then passes to the underback, fire coppers, and hop back, all of which are in a separate building; it is then pumped up to the cooler and passes through the refrigerator to the fermenting tuns, and to the racking back. The hop and malt stores are conveniently placed.

24-Quarter Brewery. (Plate VII.)

Cold and hot liquor backs fixed at top of the building. Malt is conveyed from the stores by a screw into the malt hopper, then over the screen through the rolls into grist case; there are two mash tuns with mashing machines; the wort then runs into the underback, and out to the steam coppers into the hop back, from which it is pumped up to the coolers, passing through the refrigerators to the fermenting tuns and cleansing room, either to the loading stage or cellars. The hop store is placed next the tun room, the coppers and boilers are in a separate building on the ground floor.

40-Quarter Brewery. (Plates VIII. and IX.)

Cold liquor back is fixed outside the brewery, hot liquor copper underneath, heated by fire. Malt is pulled up by steam tackle, and after passing over the screen and through the rolls, is taken up by the elevator to the grist case, to which is fixed a Steel's machine serving the two tuns; it then runs into the underback, and is afterwards pumped up to the small top back, and runs into the fire coppers, passing from thence to the hop back, coolers, refrigerator, and fermenting tuns to the cleansing room ready to send out.

It is to be observed this was a special arrangement to suit circumstances, and not exactly the plan we should have carried out in an ordinary case.

40-Quarter Brewery. (Plates X. and XI.)

Cold liquor back in this case forms part of the roof of the brewery; the hot liquor back, heated by a steam coil, is fixed in the corner over the mash tuns. Malt is hoisted by steam tackle and thrown into the hopper, passing over the screen and through the rolls to the elevator, which lifts up the grist to screw conveying it to the grist case. Willison's mashing machine is fixed to the outlet serving the two tuns, each of which is fitted with internal machines driven from shafting under the tuns. The wort runs into the underback, fitted with steam coil, and then to fire coppers, running out into hop back, being then pumped up to the coolers, through the refrigerators to the fermenting tuns and "unions," and then to racking backs. The beer is raised from the cellar by steam power to the loading floor, at about the level of drays, &c. The coppers, boilers, hop back, &c., are in a separate building.

70-QUARTER BREWERY. (Plates XII. and XIII.)

Cold and hot liquor backs fixed at top, the latter heated by steam coil. Malt is conveyed from the malt stores by a screw into the malt hopper, passing over the screen and through the rolls; the grist is taken up by an elevator to the grist case. There are two mash tuns fitted with mashing machines. The wort goes out into the underback and fire coppers, then into the hop back, and then pumped up to the coolers and through refrigerator to the fermenting tuns and "unions," and lastly to the racking rounds and beer store. The casks are raised from this store by steam power.

The coppers and boilers are in a separate building on the ground floor.

160-QUARTER BREWERY. (Plates XIV. and XV.)

Cold liquor back is fixed near the roof; the hot liquor backs are copper fitted with patent steam coils.

Malt is pulled up into the stores by steam tackle from the bins, and by means of a screw and elevator taken to the measurer; it then passes to the malt hopper, and over the screen to the rolls; a screw takes the grist to the grist cases. Two Steel's mashing machines are fitted to the outlets, serving four mash tuns; these are fitted with gun-metal mashing machines and gun-metal false bottoms. The wort then passes to the underback, into the fire coppers, and afterwards pumped up to the coolers, passing through the refrigerator to the fermenting tuns and "unions," which command the racking rounds. The casks after filling are lowered to the cellars, from which they are raised by a steam cask hoist, and loaded out direct into the railway trucks, the floors of which are level with the loading-out floor. The brewer's room is upon the mash-tun stage. The boilers and coppers are in a separate building; the railway trucks run direct into this part and deliver the coals at the copper side.

German Brewery. (Plates XVI. and XVII.)

Section through a brewery as arranged for brewing on the ordinary German system.

The section is not drawn to a scale, and is given as the usual type.

A, malt rolls; B, grist case; C, external mashing machine; D, first mash tun fitted with an internal mashing machine, but no false bottom; E, first copper fitted with rouser; F, pump for raising the "thick-mash" from copper to mash tun; G, second pump for pumping mash into the second mash tun H, which tun would be fitted with mashing machine and false bottom; K, second copper; L, hop back; M, pump for raising wort to coolers, &c.

The brewing process would be as follows: After grinding, the first mash would be made by means of the external mashing machine C with cold water; at the same time a certain quantity of water is being boiled in the copper E, which is afterwards pumped up into the mash tun, and the internal mashing machine is started. After remaining in the tun a short time, about half the mash is run into the copper E, and gradually raised to boiling point, which is afterwards pumped back into tun D and mashed again. The "goods" are then pumped into second mash tun H, and the clear wort run off into copper K; the sparger is then started until the "length" is made up, the hops are added at different times and in various quantities, according to quality of beer to be produced, the whole process taking from fifteen to eighteen hours.

As the success of the German system depends on the fermentation, great attention has been given to the construction of the tun rooms; the plan given is the one now generally adopted. The space round the cellar is for storing ice, so as to keep the temperature at about 34°; the tuns being also fitted with floating attemperators charged with ice.

100-Quarter Malting. (Plates XVIII. and XIX.)

We have described this generally at p. 117, under the head of "Cost of Erection"; we add some few details here.

The kiln floor is constructed with perforated tiles resting on iron joists. The working floors are of tiles laid in cement on a wood floor; sometimes they rest on concrete arches.

German Malting. (Plate XX.)

The cistern and working floors are much the same as above described. The drawing shows the kiln with two drying floors above, the heat being diffused by the channels like a cross perforated at the sides.

TABLES AND USEFUL MEMORANDA.

SUNDRY WEIGHTS AND MEASURES.

Quarter of Malt	=	10·24	cube feet.
When ground	=	12·	cube feet nearly.
Bushel of Malt	=	1·28	cube feet,
		or 2218·2	cube inches.

Quarter of Malt weighs about 3 cwt.

1 Butt	=	108 Gallons	=	432 Quarts	=	864 Pints.
1 Puncheon	=	72 „	=	288 „	=	576 „
1 Hogshead	=	54 „	=	216 „	=	532 „
1 Barrel	=	36 „	=	144 „	=	288 „
1 Kilderkin	=	18 „	=	72 „	=	144 „
1 Firkin	=	9 „	=	36 „	=	72 „

1 Barrel = 5·77 cube feet nearly,
or 9971 „ inches.

1 Gallon = ·16 „ feet.
277 „ inches.

1 Gallon of distilled water = 10 lb.

SIZE OF LONDON CASKS.

	Length of Stave.	Diameter at Head.	Diameter at Centre.
Butt,	52 inches.	26 inches.	33½ inches.
Puncheon,	42½ „	25 „	31 „
Hogshead,	37½ „	23½ „	28 „
Barrel,	32 „	21 „	25 „
Kilderkin,	25½ „	17 „	20 „

FOREIGN MEASURES COMPARED WITH ENGLISH.

	Foreign.		English. Gals.	English. Quarts.
America	Gallon	=	..	3·33
Austria	Eimer	=	12	1·85
Denmark	Anker	=	8	2
France	Litre	=	..	·88
Germany	Eimer	=	15	·06
Russia	Veddras	=	2	2·8
Sweden	Eimer	=	17	1·2

FRENCH MEASURES.

LINEAR, OR MEASURES OF LENGTH.

		Mètres.		Inches.		Feet.
Millimètre	=	·001	=	·03937	=	·00328
Centimètre	=	·01	=	·3937	=	·0328
Decimètre	=	·1	=	3·937	=	·328
*Mètre**	=	1·0	=	39·37079	=	3·2809
Decamètre	=	10·0	=	..	=	32·809
Hectomètre	=	100·0	=	..	=	328·09
Kilomètre	=	1000·0	=	..	=	3280·9
Myriamètre	=	10000·0	=	..	=	32809·0

* The basis or unit of the system is the mètre, the length of which, in English measure, is 1·0936 yards, or 3·2809 feet, or 39·371 inches. By *multiplying* the mètre respectively by 10, 100, 1000, and 10,000, we obtain the *deca*, *hecto*, *kilo*, and *myriamètre* respectively; and by *dividing* the mètre by 10, 100, and 1000, the *deci*, *centi*, and *millimètre* respectively are obtained.

The following are the English equivalents—

0·025 Mètres	=	1 inch.
0·304 ,,	=	1 foot.
0·914 ,,	=	1 yard.
1609·31 ,,	=	1 mile.
6·444 sq. Centimètres	=	1 sq. inch.
0·092 sq. Mètres	=	1 sq. foot.
0·83 sq. ,,	=	1 sq. yard.

SUPERFICIAL OR MEASURE OF SURFACE.

1 Milliare	=	155· sq. inches.
1 Centiare	=	10·764 sq. feet.
1 Deciare	=	11·96 sq. yards.
1 *Are**	=	119·6 ,,
1 Decare	=	1196 ,,
1 Hectare	=	2·472 sq. acres.

* The unit of square measure is equal to 1 square decamètre.

MEASURES OF SOLIDITY.

1 Millistere*	=	01·028 cubic inches.
1 Centiare	=	610·28 „
1 Decistere	=	3·53170 cubic feet.
1 Decastere	=	13·08 cubic yards.
1 Hectostere	=	130·8 „
1 Kilostere	=	1308·0 „

* A *stere*, the unit of solid measure, is equal to 1 cubic mètre, or 35·317 cubic feet.

16·3052 cubic centimètres	=	1 cubic inch English.
28·314 cubic decimètres	=	1 cubic foot „
764·58 „	=	1 cubic yard „

MEASURES OF WEIGHT.

1 Milligramme	=	·015434	grains (Troy).
1 Centigramme	=	·15434	„
1 Decigramme	=	1·5434	„
1 *Gramme**	=	15·434	„
1 Decagramme	=	154·3	„
1 Hectogramme	=	3·527	ounces (avoir.).
1 Kilogramme	=	2·2048	lb. „
1 Myriagramme	=	22·048	lb. „

* The *Gramme* unit of weight is equal to a "cubic" centimètre of distilled water, in vacuo at its maximum density, or 390 degrees Fahrenheit.

MEASURES OF CAPACITY.

1 Millilitre	=	·06102 cubic inches.
1 Centilitre	=	·61028 „
1 Decilitre	=	6·1028 „
1 *Litre**	=	61·028 „
1 Decalitre	=	610·2 cubic inches, or 2·2 imperial gals.
1 Hectolitre	=	3·531 cubic feet, or 2·75 „ bushels.
1 Kilolitre	=	35·317 „
1 Myrialitre	=	353·17 „

* The unit of the measure of capacity is equal to 1 cubic decimètre, or 61·028 cubic inches, or 1·761 imperial pints.

·55 cubic decimètres	=	1 pint (imperial).
4·404 ,,	=	1 gallon ,,
35·238 ,,	=	1 bushel ,,
28·338 grammes *	=	1 ounce (avoir.).
0·453 kilogrammes	=	1 pound ,,
50·796 ,,	=	1 cwt. ,,
1015·938 ,,	=	1 ton ,,

* To change *grammes into pounds* (avoirdupois), multiply the number of grammes by ·0022. To change *kilogrammes into cwts.*, we have to multiply by 0·1969. To change *pounds* (English) *into kilogrammes* (French), multiply by 0·4535. To change *gallons into litres*, multiply by 4·543. To change *cubic inches into litres*, multiply by ·0163.

WEIGHT OF A SQUARE FOOT IN LB.

Thickness.	Iron.	Brass.	Copper.	Lead.	Zinc.
1/8	5·0	5·5	5·8	7·4	4·7
1/4	10·0	11·0	11·6	14·8	9·4
3/8	15·0	16·4	17·2	22·2	14·0
1/2	20·0	21·9	22·9	29·5	18·7
5/8	25·0	27·4	28·6	36·9	23·4
3/4	30·0	32·9	34·3	44·3	28·1
7/8	35·0	38·3	40·0	51·7	32·8
1 in.	40·0	43·9	45·8	59·1	37·5

WEIGHT OF COPPER PIPES IN LB. PER FOOT.

Internal Diameter.	1/4 in. thick.	3/16 thick.	1/8 thick.	1/16 thick.
3 in.	9·85	7·24	4·72	2·2
2½ ,,	8·31	6·12	3·96	1·93
2 ,,	6·81	5·01	3·21	1·55
1½ ,,	5·29	3·85	2·43	1·15
1 ,,	3·76	2·60	1·69	·78

COMPARATIVE HEAT-CONDUCTING POWER OF VARIOUS METALS.

Gold	1·00	Iron	·34
Silver	·97	Tin	·31
Copper ..	·89	Lead	·18
Zinc	·37		

WEIGHT PER LINEAL FOOT OF ROUND AND SQUARE WROUGHT-IRON SHAFTING IN LB.

Diameter.	Round.	Square.	Diameter.	Round.	Square.
$1\frac{1}{2}$	5·91	7·52	$3\frac{1}{2}$	32·35	41·21
2	10·53	13·42	4	42·27	53·83
$2\frac{1}{2}$	16·48	21·01	$4\frac{1}{2}$	53·51	68·15
3	23·75	30·26	5	66·08	84·15

WEIGHTS OF VARIOUS MATERIALS.

Water.—A cubic inch weighs ·0361 lb.; a gallon, 10 lb.; a cubic foot, 62·32 lb.; or measures, say, $6\frac{1}{4}$ gallons. *Stones.*—Craigleith, one ton equal to 14·75 cubic feet; granite, 13·5 cubic feet to the ton; Bath, 16 cubic feet to the ton; Portland stone, 14·75 cubic feet to the ton; Yorkshire, 14·5 cubic feet to the ton; marble, 13·5. *Paving-stones.*—Granite, 3 inches thick, 54 superficial feet to the ton; Yorkshire, 3 inches thick, $57\frac{1}{2}$ superficial feet to the ton, or 39 lb. to the foot superficial; Purbeck, 3 inches thick, 55·25 superficial feet to the ton, or $40\frac{1}{2}$ lb. to the foot superficial; marble slabs, $2\frac{1}{2}$ inches thick, weigh nearly 36 lb. to the foot superficial. *Limes and Cements.*—Lime, in the stone, weighs 75 lb. to the bushel, and 59 lb. to the cubic foot; in ground state, 63 and 49 respectively; Portland cement, 100 to 112 lb. to the bushel, 75 lb. to the cubic foot. *Bricks.*—London stock-brick, size, $8\frac{3}{4}$ inches long, $4\frac{1}{4}$ broad, by $2\frac{3}{4}$ deep, one thousand = 3 tons, each brick weighs nearly 7 lb. *Tiles.*—Pan tiles for roofing, size, $13\frac{1}{2}$ inches long, $9\frac{1}{2}$ broad, and $\frac{1}{2}$ inch thick, weigh each $5\frac{1}{4}$ lb., and 2 tons 7 cwt. to the 1000; paving tiles, 6 inches square by 1 inch thick, weigh $2\frac{1}{2}$ lb., and 19·25 cwt. to the 1000. *Slates.*—Per 1000, 'duchesses,' 3 tons; 'countesses,' 2 tons; 'ladies,' $1\frac{1}{4}$ ton; 'doubles,' $\frac{3}{4}$ of a ton. Taking them in this order, the weight of slates necessary to cover a 'square' of roof, or 100 feet superficial, is 6 cwt., $6\frac{3}{4}$ cwt., and $7\frac{1}{2}$ cwt. *Corrugated Iron.*—The weight per 'square' of the thickness of No. 22 Birmingham wire gauge, is 1 cwt. 2 qrs. 7 lb.; No. 20 Birmingham wire gauge, 1 cwt. 3 qrs. 6 lb.; No. 18 Birmingham wire gauge, 2 cwt. 1 qr. 6 lb.; No. 16 Birmingham wire gauge, 3 cwt. 14 lb. *Timber.*—

English oak weighs 50 lb. to the cubic foot; American oak, 47; Baltic, 46; mahogany, Honduras, 40; and mahogany, Spanish, 55 lb. Larch, 35; ash, 50; birch, 48; beech, 51; elm, 39; poplar, 32; red pine, 40; yellow pine, 33; Dantzic fir, 35; Memel fir, 38 lb. to the cubic foot.

THERMOMETER.

Freezing point, Centigrade and Réaumur 0°, in Fahrenheit 32°.

Boiling point, Centigrade 100°, Réaumur 80°, Fahrenheit 212°.

Formula, to convert degrees of Centigrade and Réaumur into degrees Fahrenheit, when above freezing point, $32° + \frac{C° \times 9}{5} =$ degrees Fahrenheit; $32° + \frac{R° \times 9}{4} =$ degrees Fahrenheit. When below freezing point, but above zero, on the Fahrenheit scale, deduct the fraction from 32° instead of adding.

For converting degrees Fahrenheit into degrees of Centigrade or Réaumur, if above freezing point,

$$(F - 32) \times \frac{4}{9} = R°. \qquad (F - 32) \times \frac{5}{9} = C°.$$

If below freezing point,

$$(32 - F) \times \frac{4}{9} = -R°. \qquad (32 - F) \times \frac{5}{9} = -C°.$$

EXPLANATION OF TABLE No. I.,

For Calculating Contents in Barrels of Circular Vessels.

If the diameter of the vessel is given in the table, the quantity opposite to that dimension is the contents for every foot in depth of the vessel.

If, however, the exact dimension is not found, take the nearest dimension to it, and multiply the difference given in the second column by the number of inches the diameter exceeds the nearest dimension, and add the two together—the result giving the contents per foot in depth.

Example No. 1.—Required the contents of a circular vessel 10′ 8″ in diameter, and 6 feet deep. The contents of a vessel 10′ 6″ in diameter, according to table is, ... 14·99 barrels,

multiply the difference, ·2433 by 2 inches, and add to former amount, ... } .. ·4866

Contents for every foot in depth of the vessel 10′ 8″ in diameter, ... } = 15·4766

This multiplied by the depth, 6 feet, is equal to 15·4766 by 6 = 92·8596 barrels.

Example No. 2.—Required the contents of a vessel 12′ 0″ in diameter, and 6 feet deep. According to table, the contents per foot of a vessel 12 feet in diameter is 19·58. This multiplied by 6 feet (the depth) = 117·48 barrels.

Table No. I., for Calculating the Contents of Circular Vessels into Barrels.

Diameter.	Contents in Barrels per Foot in Depth.	Add per In. in Diameter.	Diameter.	Contents in Barrels per Foot in Depth.	Add per In. in Diameter.
3″	0084	·0085	10′ 0″	13·59	·2333
6″	·0339	·0141	10′ 6″	14·99	·2433
9″	·0764	·0198	11′ 0″	16·45	·2550
1′ 0″	·1359	·0283	11′ 6″	17·98	·2666
1′ 6″	·3059	·0396	12′ 0″	19·58	·2766
2′ 0″	·5438	·0526	12′ 6″	21·24	·2883
2′ 6″	·8597	·0600	13′ 0″	22·97	·3016
3′ 0″	1·22	·0733	13′ 6″	24·78	·3116
3′ 6″	1·66	·0850	14′ 0″	26·65	·3216
4′ 0″	2·17	·0966	14′ 6″	28·58	·3350
4′ 6″	2·75	·1066	15′ 0″	30·59	·3450
5′ 0″	3·39	·1183	15′ 6″	32·66	·3583
5′ 6″	4·10	·1311	16′ 0″	34·81	·3666
6′ 0″	4·89	·1416	16′ 6″	37·01	·3800
6′ 6″	5·74	·1533	17′ 0″	39·29	·3916
7′ 0″	6·66	·1633	17′ 6″	41·64	·4016
7′ 6″	7·64	·1783	18′ 0″	44·05	·4133
8′ 0″	8·71	·1850	18′ 6″	46·53	·4250
8′ 6″	9·82	·1983	19′ 0″	49·08	·4366
9′ 0″	11·01	·2100	19′ 6″	51·70	·4483
9′ 6″	12·27	·2200	20′ 0″	54·39	

EXPLANATION OF TABLE No. II.

To find the contents of square vessels, if the length is given at the top of the table, and the width at the side, the amount given at the intersection of the two columns is the contents in barrels for every foot in depth of a square vessel that size.

Example.—Required the contents of a vessel 12 feet long, 6 feet wide, and 3 feet deep.

Find the column with 12 feet at the top, and find the amount in that column opposite to the 6 feet, at side of table, which is 12·46; this multiplied by the depth, viz. 3 feet, gives 37·38 barrels as the contents of the vessel.

Second Case.—If the exact dimension of the length is not given in table, but the dimension of the width is given, take the next lowest, as in preceding example, and multiply the decimal given at the right hand of the table, and opposite to the required width, by the number of inches the width exceeds the given dimensions, and add to the amount given in the table.

Example.—Required the contents of a vessel 11′ 8″ × 7′ 0″ × 3 feet deep.

First find the contents of a vessel 11′ 0″ × 7′ 0″, as in preceding example, ... = 13·34

Then multiply the decimal given ·101 in right-hand column by 8 inches, being the number of inches the dimension exceeds that given in the table, ... = ·808

Contents in barrels per foot in depth, ... 14·148

Then 14·148 × 3 feet (the depth) = 42·444 barrels as the total contents of the vessel.

Third Case.—When neither the exact dimensions of the length or width is to be found in table, find the contents of the next lowest dimensions, as in first case; multiply the decimal opposite to the width by the number of inches the length exceeds the dimension given in table, and also multiply the decimal given at the foot of column by the number of inches the width exceeds that given in table; add the three amounts together, and the result will give the contents of the vessel in barrels for every foot in depth.

Example.—Required the contents of a vessel 13 feet 3 inches long × 7 feet 8 wide × 3 feet deep.

First, Find the contents of a vessel 13′ 0″ × 7′ 6″ as given in table, ... = 16·88

Second, Multiply ·108, as given at right hand of table, by 3, as the length exceeds that given in the table by that amount, ... = ·324

Third, Multiply ·188, as given at foot of column, by 2, as the width exceeds that given in the tables by that amount, ... = ·376

17·580

The result being the contents in barrels for every foot in depth.

∴ 1·7580 × 3 (the given depth) = 52.74 barrels as the total contents.

TABLE No. II., FOR CALCULATING THE CONTENTS IN BARRELS OF SQUARE VESSELS.

	5 ft.	6 ft.	7 ft.	8 ft.	9 ft.	10 ft.	11 ft.	12 ft.	13 ft.	14 ft.	15 ft.	Add per Inch.
5′ 0″	4·332	5·19	6·06	6·93	7·79	8·66	9·53	10·39	11·25	12·12	12·99	·072
5′ 6″	4·76	5·71	6·66	7·62	8·57	9·52	10·47	11·43	12·37	13·33	14·28	·079
6′ 0″	5·19	6·23	7·27	8·31	9·35	10·39	11·42	12·46	13·50	14·54	15·58	·086
6′ 6″	5·63	6·75	7·88	9·00	10·13	11·26	12·38	13·51	14·63	15·76	16·88	·093
7′ 0″	6·06	7·27	8·49	9·70	10·91	12·13	13·34	14·55	15·76	16·98	18·19	·101
7′ 6″	6·49	7·79	9·09	10·39	11·69	12·99	14·29	15·58	16·88	18·18	19·48	·108
8′ 0″	6·93	8·31	9·70	11·08	12·47	13·86	15·24	16·63	18·01	19·40	20·78	·115
8′ 6″	7·36	8·84	10·31	11·78	13·26	14·73	16·20	17·67	19·14	20·62	22·09	·123
9′ 0″	7·79	9·35	10·91	12·47	14·03	15·59	17·15	18·70	20·26	21·82	23·38	·129
9′ 6″	8·23	9·87	11·52	13·16	14·81	16·46	18·10	19·75	21·39	23·04	24·68	·137
10′ 0″	8·66	10·39	12·13	13·86	15·50	17·33	19·06	20·79	22·52	24·26	25·99	·144
10′ 6″	9·09	10·91	12·73	14·55	16·37	18·19	20·01	21·82	23·64	25·46	27·28	·151
11′ 0″	9·53	11·43	13·34	15·24	17·15	19·06	20·96	22·87	24·77	26·68	28·59	·159
11′ 6″	9·76	11·95	13·95	15·94	17·93	19·93	21·92	23·91	25·90	27·90	29·89	·166
12′ 0″	10·39	12·47	14·55	16·63	18·71	20·80	22·86	24·94	27·02	29·10	31·18	·173
12′ 6″	10·83	12·99	15·16	17·32	19·49	21·66	23·82	25·99	28·15	30·32	32·48	·180
13′ 0″	11·26	13·51	15·77	18·02	20·27	22·52	24·78	27·03	29·28	31·54	33·79	·187
13′ 6″	11·69	14·03	16·37	18·71	21·05	23·39	25·72	28·06	30·40	32·75	35·08	·195
14′ 0″	12·13	14·55	16·98	19·40	21·83	24·26	26·68	29·11	31·53	33·96	36·38	·202
14′ 6″	12·56	15·07	17·59	20·10	22·61	25·13	27·64	30·15	32·66	35·18	37·69	·209
15′ 0″	12·99	15·59	18·19	20·79	23·39	25·99	28·58	31·18	33·70	36·38	38·98	·216
15′ 6″	13·43	16·11	18·80	21·48	24·17	26·86	29·54	32·23	34·91	37·60	40·28	·224
16′ 0″	13·86	16·33	19·41	22·18	24·95	27·73	30·50	33·27	36·04	38·82	41·59	·231
Add per Inch.	·071	·086	·101	·116	·130	·145	·160	·174	·188	·203	·218	

EXCISE LICENCES.

BREWERS OF BEER FOR SALE.

For and upon every licence taken out yearly by any Brewer of Beer for sale.

	£	s.	d.
Brewers (United Kingdom) for annual licence to brew beer for sale (not being black or spruce beer). If the quantity brewed within a year ending the 30th September next preceding the taking out of such licence shall not exceed 50 barrels	0	12	6
For every 50 barrels and part of 50 over and above the first 50 barrels, the additional sum of ..	0	12	6
Beginners	0	12	6
And to pay such additional sum within 10 days after the expiration of licence, as with the duty, 12*s.* 6*d.*, shall amount to the duty chargeable on a licence for a quantity of beer equal to the quantity brewed by him during the existence of his licence.			
Brewers using sugar	1	0	0
Retail brewers, England and Scotland, retailers of beer not to be consumed on the premises	5	10	3

MALTSTERS.

	£	s.	d.
If the quantity of malt made within the year ending the 5th July shall not exceed 50 quarters	0	7	10½
Exceeding 50 and not exceeding 100 „	0	15	9
„ 100 „ 150 „	1	3	7½
„ 150 „ 200 „	1	11	6
„ 200 „ 250 „	1	19	4½
„ 250 „ 300 „	2	7	3
„ 300 „ 350 „	2	15	1½
„ 350 „ 400 „	3	3	0
„ 400 „ 450 „	3	10	10½
„ 450 „ 500 „	3	18	9
„ 500 „ 550 „	4	6	7½
550	4	14	6
Maltroasters	20	0	0
Malt made in the United Kingdom, except when made from bere or bigg only, per bushel .. .. and 5 per cent.	0	2	7
Malt made from bere or bigg only, in Scotland and Ireland, for home consumption, per bushel .. and 5 per cent.	0	2	0

PATENTS RELATING TO MALT AND HOPS: THEIR TREATMENT AND SUBSTITUTES.

1635. July 23.—85. Nicholas Halse.
Making kilns for drying malt and hops with seacoal turf, or other fuel, without touching smoke; capable also of being used for cooking, drying, and starching at one time with one fire, and thereby lessening the consumption of wood and straw.

1637. Feb. 7.—102. Thomas, Earl of Berks.
Kiln for drying malt, grain, and hops.

1698. Nov. 28.—358. J. Groves and T. Reeve.
Drying malt on iron, or tinned iron, with half the usual consumption of fuel, and with a saving of time.

1713. Dec. 1.—394. M. Bird.
Engine for drying malt and hops.

1720. May 10.—429. J. Busby.
Kiln for drying malt with hot air.

„ June 25.—430. J. T. Desagulier, D. Niblet, and W. Vreem.
Making the steam of boiling liquors useful for drying malt and hops.

1729. Aug. 7.—513. J. Allen.
Drying malt.

1745. April 18.—612. J. Kay and J. Stell.
Kiln for drying malt.

1753. Nov. 17.—594. J. Southgate.
Bringing malt liquor to much greater perfection, by means of floors of brass, copper, and lead, for curing and preparing malt.

1768. Mar. 14.—896. A. Meikle and R. Mackell.
Machine for dressing and cleansing malt.

1769. Feb. 21.—918. S. Willday.
Machine for drying malt, with coal or other fuel, without communicating any unpleasant taste or flavour to the malt.

1783. Nov. 14.—1395. R. Clark.
Malt and oat kiln of cast metal.

1796. June 9.—2116. J. Pepper.
Kiln for drying malt.

1805. Jan. 29.—2816. J. Barrett.
Construction of malt kilns, so as to prevent damages from fire, and save fuel in the drying of malt.

1807. Dec. 19.—3093. S. Salter.
Apparatus for drying malt or hops, or any kinds of grain.

1811. Nov. 26.—3509. J. Adam.
Drying malt.

1817. Mar. 28.—4112. D. Wheeler.
Method of drying and preparing malt.

„ June 10.—4133. T. Whittle and G. Eyton.
Kiln for drying malt and other substances.

1818. May 5.—4254. W. Bush.
Drying and preparing malt.

1829. July 9.—5816. T. Salmon.
Malt kiln.

1833. Sept. 7.—6468. R. Else.
Drying malt.

1837. Apr. 18.—7347. C. Farina.
Obtaining fermentable matter from grain, and manufacturing the same for various purposes.

„ Aug. 24.—7420. T. Du Boulay, J. J. C. Sheridan.
Drying and screening malt.

1841. April 5.—8921. W. L. Tizard.
Apparatus for brewing.

1842. Sept. 22.—9475. P. Stead.
Manufacture of malt.

1843. Mar. 1.—9648. G. Bell.
Machines for drying malt and other substances.

„ May 25.—9736. A. Poole.
Drying malt and grain.

„ June 10.—9767. S. J. Knight.
Kilns for drying hops, malt, and other substances.

1845. Jan. 11.—10,459. G. Bell.
Drying malt.

1849. Jan. 23.—12,439. R. Johnson.
Manufacture of malted grain—machinery connected with the process of brewing.

1851. Sept. 4.—12,735. B. Hallewell.
Drying malt.

1852. May 8.—14,119. W. L. Tizard.
Machinery, apparatus, and processes for the preparation of grain, and its conversion into liquors, whether malt, saccharine, vinous, alcoholic, or acetous.

„ Dec. 21.—1125. E. D. Moore.
Preparation of malt and hops.

1853. Jan. 14.—97. J. Lillie.
Machinery to be used in the process of malting, drying, and seasoning grain, including certain vegetable and other substances.

1854. Feb. 28.—490. T. J. Johnson.
Apparatus for roasting malt.

„ April 28.—963. W. L. Tizard.
Apparatus applicable to the drying and roasting of malt and other vegetable substances.

„ May 18.—1113. J. C. Robertson.
Preparation and roasting of coffee and other substances (malt).

„ Dec. 27.—2726. J. Nash.
Means or process of drying malt, grain, or roots.

1855. Nov. 19.—2600. J. Fleetwood.
Portable apparatus for making malt, and for drying hops, corn, and other grains and seeds.

1856. Feb. 26.—494. R. A. Brooman (A. Bochler and P. F. Quantin).
A composition, or compositions, to be used as a substitute for hops in brewing.

„ Aug. 6.—1855. W. Watt.
Treating or preparing Indian corn and other grain for fermentation and distillation.

„ Oct. 16.—2415. A. Tooth.
An improved process for bleaching malt, whereby the colour is rendered more suitable for the brewing of pale or bright malt liquors.

„ Nov. 21.—2766. C. Garton and J. S. and G. Parsons.
A method of treating cane sugar, in order to fit it to be employed in brewing and distilling.

1857. Jan. 10.—94. W. Watt.
Treating or preparing Indian corn and other grain, and any amylaceous vegetable substances for fermentation and distillation.

„ „ 30.—276. A. Wright.
An improved manufacture of malt.

„ Feb. 28.—585. E. and M. A. Heale.
Treatment of vegetable and other substances (drying hay, hops, &c.).

„ Sept. 18.—2419. D. Junhof.
Machinery adapted to the exhausting or forcing of air, gases, or vapour; application of such machinery to various useful purposes (for drying malt).

„ Oct. 14.—2632. J. C. Blomley.
An improved method of drying malt, hops, and other produce.

„ Nov. 11.—2845. P. Madden.
Kilns for drying corn, malt, or other granular substances, partly applicable to the screening or sifting of such substances during the process of drying.

1858. Aug. 31.—1981. P. D. Margesson.
Improvements in treating sugar canes, &c.; also in manufacturing sugar and worts or wash for brewing, distilling, and vinegar making.

1859. Feb. 18.—451. C. Garton.
An improved method of treating cane sugar in order to render it fitter to be employed in brewing, distilling, and wine and vinegar making.

„ April 21.—999. A. F. Vanhulst.
An improved kiln for drying malt.

„ May 11.—1178. A. Manbré.
An improved method of extracting and purifying sugar called glucose from potatoes, or starch, or dextrine, for the purposes and uses of brewers, &c.

„ Sept. 2.—2005. S. D. Goff, H. Davis, S. Strangman, and E. Strangman.
An improved method of and apparatus for drying malt, corn, and other articles.

1860. Oct. 10.—2461. S. Barnet.
Machinery for drying grain, roots, and seeds, and for roasting coffee, cocoa, chicory, malt, and other vegetable substances.

„ Dec. 10.—R. Davison.
Apparatus for drying and heating (applicable to the drying of malt, hops, or grain).

1861. Feb. 12.—358. W. Maltby.
Improvements in the process of manufacturing of glutinous or viscous substance to be used in brewing and distilling, and also in the apparatus to be used for the same and similar purposes.

„ Sept. 26.—2407. J. Sessier.
Improved means of treating barley, corn, and other cereals for brewing and other purposes.

„ Nov. 7.—2798. H. G. Gibson (J. Perrigault).
Apparatuses for drying hops, malt, grain, and other vegetable substances, part of which is applicable as a fan or blower.

„ Dec. 12.—3118. A. Tonnar.
Method of and apparatus for drying and cleansing malt, as well as any other species of grain and seed intended for brewing, distilling, and agricultural purposes.

1862. May 2.—1295. R. Walker.
Improvements in malting, and in apparatus therefor.

„ „ 12.—1429. A. B. Freeland.
Preparation or treatment of hops.

1862. May 19.—1516. Morris, Weare, and Monckton.
Obtaining and applying light and heat by electricity. (Heat for Malting.)
„ Sept. 3.—2434. C. Garton.
An improved method of applying heat in the manufacture and refining of sugar, and in malting, hop drying, brewing, distilling, and vinegar making.
1863. Mar. 2.—584. C. Garton.
Ditto. ditto.
„ „ 14.—698. R. Moreland, jun.
Apparatus for making extracts of hops, and for selecting or separating the seeds and pollen from hops.
„ April 7.—376. J. H. Johnson.
Machinery or apparatus for drying grain, applicable also to the manufacture of malt.
„ June 9.—1428. G. Hills.
Obtaining certain products from hops.
„ „ 19.—1539. J. Watts.
Machinery or apparatus for the manufacture of malt.
„ „ „ —1542. M. Henry.
Improvements in decorticating grain and seeds, and in the application of the products obtained by, and materials used in, decorticating.
„ Aug. 13.—1997. J. Ellis.
Machinery for scouring, cleaning, and polishing wheat, rice, malt, grain, and other seeds.
„ Oct. 22.—2602. J. Weems.
Machinery, apparatus, or means for drying, cleaning, and cooling grain and other vegetable products (malt).
„ Dec. 11.—3124. A. Epps.
Improvements in malt and hop kilns, which improvements are partly applicable to the ventilation and warming of buildings, and to the drying of various substances.
1864. Sept. 6.—2177. D. Walker.
Arrangements for malting.
1865. Dec. 1.—3087. W. R. Taylor.
Improvements in the treatment of grain, and in the process of malting, and in the apparatus employed therein.
1866. Apr. 23.—R. W. Abbots.
Fireplaces or furnaces of malt and other kilns.
„ May 1.—1235. F. Grilton.
Apparatus for treating malt.
„ June 6.—1559. W. Lawrence.
Improvements in the manufacture of malt, and in apparatus for drying malt and hops.
„ Nov. 23.—3803. R. Potter, M.A.
Process of cleansing, purifying, and bleaching various kinds of grain-making malt.
„ Dec. 29.—3422. J. Slatter.
An improved screen or sifter for screening cinders, corn, tea, sugar, gravel, malt, and other granular substances.
1867. Jan. 9.—57. R. Winder.
Improved machinery for pocketing hops, &c.
„ „ 30.—249. T. Prideaux.
Improvements in the heating of malt kilns, and other apparatus of a similar character.
„ Feb. 26.—520. W. H. Samson.
Means and apparatus for drying hops.

1867. May 18.—1485. J. L. Norton.
Drying malt, and also brewers' and distillers' grains and spent hops.

„ July 17.—2095. J. Schofield and J. C. Dawson.
Improved means and apparatus for malting or drying barley, part of which means and apparatus is also applicable to other purposes.

„ „ 20.—2125. W. Taylor.
Pipes for ventilating, heating, and vaporizing hot-houses, malt-houses, and other buildings.

„ „ 22.—2132. T. A. Breithaupt.
Certain process of manufacturing extract and essence of hops, to be substituted for the plant itself in the making of beer.

„ Oct. 5.—2804. J. S. Williamson.
An improved apparatus for drying corn, malt, and other similar substances.

„ „ 23.—2976. T. Welton.
Ozonized or oxygenated bread, biscuits, cakes, and other substances (barley in malting).

„ Nov. 5.—3124. A. M'Dougall.
Improvements in apparatus for stirring or agitating solid substances, and for exposing them to the action of the air, gases, and vapours.

1868. May 23.—1701. W. Seck.
Kilns or apparatus applicable to the drying or treating of grain for the manufacture of malt.

„ Aug. 19.—2590. W. H. Davey.
Apparatus for drying linen and other fabrics or substances (drying malt).

„ Dec. 24.—3936. R. Boby.
Construction of floors for malt kilns or drying rooms.

„ „ 31.—3976. H. A. Bonneville.
A new and improved apparatus for drying and growing malt and all other grains, fruits, or vegetables.

1869. Jan. 11.—84. F. C. Matthews.
Improvements in treating Indian corn to obtain a new product applicable to brewing.

„ Feb. 22.—539. J. and W. Weems.
Improvements in machinery, apparatus, or means for malting, heating, drying, &c.

„ Mar. 10.—738. G. Spenser.
Improvements in preserving corn and other grain, beans, malt, &c.

„ June 21.—1897. A. Manbré.
Improvements in preparing and treating cereal and other vegetable substances, and converting it into fermentable saccharine.

„ July 21.—2212. J. H. Johnson.
Obtaining extracts from hops.

„ „ 22.—2227. W. A. Gilbee.
An improved method of preserving the aromatic principle of hops.

„ Oct. 22.—3073. R. J. Goodbody and R. E. Donavan.
A new or improved apparatus for roasting tobacco, malt, &c.

„ Nov. 11.—3248. J. M'Cormick.
An improvement in the process of brewing malt and other substances.

1869. Dec. 1.—3474. J. Forbes.
Improvements in desiccating malt, grain, and other similar substances.
„ „ 15.—3621. E. Moss.
Self-acting malt-drying apparatus.
„ „ 18.—3669. J. Mackenzie.
Improvements in preparing malt or grain for brewing.
1870. Jan. 22.—205. W. Garton.
Preparation of fermentable saccharine matter.
„ Mar. 15.—769. W. E. Newton.
Malt kilns.
„ May 2.—1249. S. W. Stanbridge.
Preparation of malt for brewing, colouring, flavouring, and keeping ales, &c.
„ „ 28.—1562. A. Manbré.
Improvements in apparatus applicable to the conversion of cereal substances into saccharine matter.
„ July 12.—1969. M. C. Maximas.
Improvements in drying malt.
„ „ 13.—1973. J. A. Coffey.
Improvements in process and apparatus for drying and roasting coffee, malt, &c.
„ Sept. 8.—2429. W. Silcock.
An improved screen wire for floor of kilns.
„ Nov. 8.—2943. W. E. Newton.
An improved process for extracting the useful substance of hops.
1871. May 6.—1232. W. Garton.
Improvements in the manufacture of saccharine material.
1872. Feb. 1.—329. W. R. Lake.
An improved method of preparing and pressing hops.
„ Dec. 30.—3956. J. H. Johnson.
Improvements in the treatment of maize.
1874. Jan. 5.—55. R. G. Perry.
Improvements in kilns or drying chambers.
„ Feb. 23.—678. H. B. Barlow (Galland).
Improvements in brewing and machinery employed.
„ June 8.—1988. H. B. Barlow.
An improved system of malting.
„ „ 16.—2083. J. H. Johnson.
Improvements in the preservation of hops.
„ Oct. 13.—2524. F. Wirth.
Improvements in the method of preparing malt.
„ „ 20.—3598. R. G. Perry.
Improvements in kilns or drying chambers.
„ Nov. 12.—3909. C. O. Sullivan and W. G. Valentine.
Improvements in the treatment of starch and the production thereof of a substitute for malt.
„ „ 17.—3950. W. Garton.
Improvements in the manufacture of sugar for brewing.
1875. Feb. 2.—381. J. H. Johnson.
Improvements in the treatment of farinaceous substances.
„ „ 17.—519. A. Manbré.
An improved process for treating vegetable substances.
„ Mar. 4.—810. J. H. Johnson.
Improvements in the method of the manufacture of glucose.
„ „ 24.—1083. J. N. Lessware.
Improvements in the manufacture of glucose sugar.

1875. May 8.—1724. A. Manbré.
Improvements in the manufacture of sugar.
„ „ 12.—1774. C. Richardson.
An improved method of treating and liquefying saccharine matters.
„ July 9.—2471. A. Sezille.
Improvements in the manufacture of malt.
„ Sept. 24.—3338. J. N. Lessware.
Improvements in the manufacture of glucose.
1876. Feb. 9.—519. R. Free.
Kilns for drying malt, hops, grain, &c.
„ Mar. 27.—1311. W. Garton.
Brewing, and the preparation of a material to be employed therein.
„ April 22.—1714. A. Blake.
Treatment of malt and other materials.
„ May 13.—2025. W. G. Valentine.
Manufacture of dextrine matter.
„ June 9.—2405. F. Wirth.
An improved malt-turning apparatus.
„ July 11.—2825. H. B. Barlow.
Improvements in malting and in apparatus employed.
„ Sept. 2.—3468. Tasker (Duprez).
Cleansing and purifying grain for brewing.
„ „ 23.—3724. Wirth (Ellenberger).
Mashing and preparing grain for brewing.
„ „ 26.—3749. A. Perry.
Improvements in kiln for drying malt.
„ Nov. 30.—4632. Scholes.
Drying malt, &c.
„ Dec. 22.—4961. Hoyne.
Forcing air through malt for drying same.
1877. Jan. 29.—381. Clark (Guardiola).
Hot-air machine for drying malt.
„ Feb. 6.—514. Gardiner.
Testing qualities of malt for brewing.
„ Mar. 24.—1161. Wise (Saladin).
Improved method, and apparatus for malting.
Vacuum apparatus for steeping grain.
„ „ 28.—1233. Perrins.
Substitute for hops.
„ June 20.—2391. Barlow (Armengaud).
Stove for drying malt.
„ „ „ —2392. Barlow (Armengaud).
Drum for use in malting.
„ Sept. 24.—3589. Lake (Brodie).
Turners for malting floors.
„ Oct. 16.—3831. Clark (Marbeau).
Malting barley, supplying air, &c.
„ Dec. 10.—4680. Southby.
Treating maize-malt for producing saccharine worts.
1878. April 13.—1485. Wirth (Marx and Co.).
Turning barley in germinating floors.
„ June 19.—2447. Wirth (Gruber).
Cylinder revolving apparatus for malting.
„ „ 27.—2587. Stewart (Barnard).
Grain separator for maltings.

1878. Aug. 8.—3135. Neal.
Machine for drying malt.

„ Oct. 3.—3896. Gretton.
Sparging apparatus for treating spent hops.

1879. Feb. 11.—531. Tizard.
Malting apparatus, &c.

„ „ 22.—720. Von Nawrocki (Scheidig).
Malting apparatus, &c.

„ Mar. 13.—999. Simon (partly commenced by N. J. Galland).
Improvements in malting and in the apparatus employed.

„ April 8.—1398. Wilson.
Improved apparatus for heating, cooling, and attemperating malt, &c.

„ June 19.—2440. Naumann and Pohl.
Improved treatment of hops for the preservation thereof.

„ „ 26.—2583. Wirth (Gruber).
Method of, and apparatus for, malting.

„ July 31.—3104. Siddeley and Dearn.
Apparatus for extracting moisture from hops, &c.

„ Aug. 12.—3230. Bruce and others.
Improvements in the treatment of dextrine-maltose, &c., and machinery for same.

„ Oct. 22.—4301. Reynolds.
Drying apparatus for malt, hops, &c.

„ „ 27.—4372. Prendergast and Free.
Improvements in the treatment of malt to facilitate its transport and preserve it in good condition.

1880. Jan. 27.—366. Bruce and others.
Improvements for manufacture of dextrine-maltose, &c.

„ May 7.—1867. Palm (Von Markhof).
A new rotary apparatus for malting.

„ „ 15.—2000. Reynolds.
Apparatus for drying malt and hops.

MALT MILLS.

1841. May 4.—8921. W. L. Tizard.
Apparatus for brewing.

1855. July 10.—1538. G. Riley.
Construction of mills for grinding malt and other substances.

1860. Dec. 11.—3034 A. J. Caull.
An improved pulverising and bruising machine.

1861. June 11.—1488. C. Stevens.
An improved crushing and pulverising machine.

„ Oct. 29.—2710. R. Gibbon.
Machinery or apparatus for preparing grain for brewers.

1872. Aug. 8.—2366. J. Lane and W. Onions.
Improvements in apparatus used for brewing.

1876. Mar. 16.—1127. Sainty and others.
Grain separator and cleaner.

„ July 20.—2957. Stidolph and others.
Cleaning and sorting grain.

„ Oct. 9.—3901. Lake (Howes).
Grain separator.

„ Nov. 6.—4282. Haddan (Barnard and Leas).
Separating, &c., grain.

„ „ 21.—4521. Clark (Clifford).
Separating and sorting grain.

1877. Feb. 24.—776. Stidolph and others.
Screens for barley, &c.
„ Nov. 21.—4364. Lake (Galt).
Screen for grain scouring machine.
„ Dec. 17.—5172. Tasker (Duprez).
Mill for crushing malt.
„ „ 24.—4891. Lake (Newall).
Roller mill with winnowing or separating device for grain.
1879. May 28.—2127. Ellison.
Machine for screening grain.
„ June 7.—2259. Handscombe and Co.
Appliance for screening, &c., grain.
„ „ 11.—2310. Benson.
Machine for purifying grain, &c.
„ „ 25.—2551. Pellenz.
Grain sorting machine.
„ Aug. 2.—3133. Bennett.
Grain cleaning machine
„ Dec. 3.—4955. Handscombe and Co.
Grain winnowing machine.
„ „ 4.—4971. Handscombe and Co.
Screening apparatus for grain.
1880. Feb. 16.—664. Lane.
Method of preventing clogging of wire, &c., or other covering of machines.
„ April 26.—1707. Reddie.
Improved apparatus for dressing crushed grain.
„ May 14.—1996. Clark (Millbank).
Improvements for grinding and purifying grain and other substances.

MALT MASHING AND MIXING, AND EXTRACTING WORTS.

1787. June 12.—1611. J. Walker.
Working and mashing malt and other articles in mash tuns.
1790. June 4.—1754. J. Long.
Utensils or methods to be employed in the essential parts of brewing good malt liquor.
1792. May 15.—1877. W. Whitemore.
Machine for mashing malt and other grain to be worked by steam, water, wind, horse, or other power.
1793. Nov. 2.—1965. E. Biley.
Machine for mashing malt in brewing.
1796. Sept. 9.—2136. T. Cooper.
Machine for mashing malt or other grain for brewing or distilling.
1797. Mar. 9.—2170. J. Silvester.
Mashing and mixing malt and grain used for brewing and distilling, by means of machinery.
„ „ „ —2171. H. Goodwyn, jun.
Machine and mashing tun for mixing and mashing malt and grain or corn, for brewing or distilling.
1798. May 8.—2236. W. Jones.
Machine for mixing meal or other substances with fluids, in order to extract more easily the spirit or essence of the malt or other substances to be acted upon.

1803. Nov. 12.—2740. R. Younger.
Extracting worts from malt, barley, and other grain or substances.

1807. April 21.—3036. A. Matterface.
Construction of a machine for mashing and mixing malt.

1808. Nov. 15.—3181. J. Dickson.
Construction of tuns.

1810. Mar. 12.—3315. T. Robinson.
Mashing machine.

„ „ 22.—3318. M. Shannon.
Brewing.

1813. Feb. 20.—3651. J. Roberts.
Concentrating or reducing such parts of malt and hops as are requisite in making ale, beer, porter, &c.

1836. Sept. 15.—7187. C. Farina.
Mashing apparatus.

1837. April 18.—7347. C. Farina.
Obtaining fermentable matter from grain.

1841. May 4.—8921. W. L. Tizard.
Apparatus for brewing.

1845. Nov. 20.—10,962. N. Chappell.
Manufacture of worts.

1849. Jan. 23.—12,439. R. Johnson.
Brewing—machinery connected with the process.

1852. Mar. 8.—14,006. J. Crockford.
Brewing, and brewing apparatus.

„ May 8.—14,119. W. L. Tizard.
Machinery, apparatus, &c., for the preparation of grain, and its conversion into liquors.

„ Aug. 26.—14,282. J. Lawrence.
Brewing apparatus.

„ Oct. 19.—14,327. J. Palin and R. W. Seivier.
Brewing.

1853. May 2.—1062. A. E. L. Bellford.
Extraction and manufacture of sugar, and saccharine matters.

„ Nov. 11.—2614. W. Steel.
Machinery or apparatus for mashing malt.

1854. June 27.—1413. C. H. Collette.
Manufacture of beer.

„ Oct. 4.—2132. J. Disher.
Mashing apparatus for brewing.

„ Nov. 10.—2387. E. Loysell.
Obtaining infusions or extracts from various substances.

1855. Jan. 15.—106. G. Riley.
An improved false bottom for brewers' mash tubs.

1856. Jan. 9.—65. J. T. Pitman.
An improved method of applying diastase and heat to the saccharification of starch.

„ Mar. 26.—728. W. E. Newton.
Macerating substances to be employed in the process of distillation.

„ Nov. 10.—2641. A. Barlow.
Mashing apparatus.

„ „ 28.—2841. P. Walker.
Brewing—machinery or apparatus employed therein.

1857. Feb. 20.—496. J. Grist.
Mash tuns and apparatus to be employed therewith, which apparatus is also applicable to the heating and keeping up of a continuous circulation of liquids in any vessel to which it may be connected.

1857. May 21.—1433. W. Blacklidge, jun., and G. Read.
Certain improvements in the construction of churns, which said improvements are also applicable to other agitating or stirring apparatus.

„ June 29.—1818. J. Lawrence.
Apparatus for brewing.

„ Aug. 17.—2186. J. Grist.
Mash tuns and apparatus to be employed therewith, which apparatus is also applicable to the heating and keeping up of a continuous circulation of liquids in any vessel to which it may be connected.

1858. June 26.—1441. W. L. Tizard.
An improved method of treating brewers' and distillers' malt or grist.

„ Aug. 3.—1759. J. Steel.
Brewing and distilling.

1859. Feb. 9.—371. E. Herring.
Mashing and fermenting of grain for the production of alcohol.

„ Mar. 17.—679. P. Larochette.
Machinery for brewing.

„ Aug. 1.—1779. J. Rowland.
An improved apparatus for mashing and mixing.

1860. Sept. 17.—2258. W. Teulon.
Brewing—apparatus employed therein.

„ „ 18.—2266. E. J. Hughes.
Brewing malt liquors—apparatus employed therein.

1861. Mar. 28.—778. W. Sorrel.
Apparatus for mashing malt.

„ Oct. 7.—2503. J. E. J. Sansum.
Improved machinery for mashing malt.

1862. May 9.—1395. J. Oxley.
Apparatus for facilitating the process of mashing and sparging in breweries and distilleries.

„ „ 19.—1510. R. Ramsden, jun.
Machinery or apparatus for mashing malt.

„ Nov. 28.—3192. S. J. Browning.
Machines to be employed in brewing.

1863. Jan. 1.—1. R. H. Collyer.
Improvements in the method of, and apparatus for, preparing materials for the manufacture of paper and similar purposes, part of the invention being also applicable to other operations in which materials are subject to the action of hot agents.

„ Feb. 17.—428. W. S. Dibb.
An improvement in brewing.

„ „ 27.—555. J. Fry.
Mashing machinery used in making fermented liquors.

„ April 29.—1083. F. Gretton.
Heating the contents of mash tuns.

„ June 11.—1448. M. Hatschek.
An improved method of mashing.

„ Aug. 17.—2037. A. M. Dearn.
A new centrifugal disc mashing machine.

„ „ 26.—2112. J. Fry.
Mashing machinery used in making fermented liquors.

„ Sept. 22.—2336. C. Maitland.
Mashing apparatus.

„ Nov. 21.—2939. D. W. Hamper.
Apparatus for mashing malt for brewing or distilling.

1863. Dec. 2.—3032. R. L. Clifton.
Apparatus used for brewing.

1864. Jan. 28.—235. J. Fry.
Improved arrangements of mechanism to be used in the mashing process when brewing or distilling.

„ Mar. 24.—745. C. Garton and T. Hill.
Mashing apparatus.

„ May 9.—1177. J. Roy.
Improvements applicable to self-acting mashing apparatus.

„ June 2.—1370. W. H. Mellor.
Self-acting mashing or saturating apparatus, for the use of brewers, distillers, and others.

„ July 23.—1841. F. Gregory.
Machinery or apparatus employed in breweries and distilleries.

„ Aug. 3.—1931. C. Garton and S. Hill.
Mashing apparatus.

1865. Feb. 21.—481. R. Willison.
Improvements in mashing machines, and in apparatus connected therewith.

„ April 29.—1204. F. Gregory.
Machinery or apparatus employed in breweries and distilleries.

1866. Mar. 28.—905. F. Ryder.
An improved apparatus for mashing malt or grain, to be used in the processes of brewing and distilling.

„ June 6.—1560. W. Lawrence.
Manufacture of, and apparatus for, the treatment of worts.

1867. April 20.—1150. J. Millward.
Brewers' mash tuns.

1868. Mar. 25.—1009. A. M'Glashan and J. Hendry.
Improved machinery or apparatus for mashing substances employed in the making of fermented liquors.

1869. April 16.—1174. F. Field.
Improvements in apparatus and machinery for mashing grain.

„ Oct. 16.—3019. F. F. Whitehurst.
Improvements in apparatus for mashing grain.

1872. July 20.—2180. P. R. Conron.
Improvements in mashing and stirring apparatus.

1873. June 9.—2042. M. Hatschek.
Improvements in mashing.

1874. Feb. 9.—508. W. Garton.
Improvement in the treatment of grains.

„ „ 23.—678. H. B. Barlow (Galland).
Improvements in brewing and machinery.

1875. May 22.—1886. A. B. Walker.
Improvements in machinery, plant, &c.

„ Dec. 14.—4328. J. Thompson.
An improved method of mashing.

1876. April 21.—1684. F. J. Smith.
Improved means and apparatus for mashing.

„ Sept. 7.—3521. Boddington.
Rousing or mixing fermented liquors.

„ Nov. 7.—4298. Southby.
Mashing machine for brewers.

1877. Feb. 6.—508. Henley.
Mixing, mashing, and saccharifying malt.

„ July 31.—2929. Smith (D'Heureuse).
Draining wort from mashing machine, &c.

1877. Aug. 25.—3226. Conradi (Von Sydso).
Steam mashing and mixing machine.
1878. July 5.—2692. Siddeley and Dearn.
Agitating wort during fermentation.
„ Nov. 11.—4566. Sorrell.
Agitators used in brewing.
„ „ 16.—4668. Clark (Feroe and Bennett).
Grain mashing process, &c., for brewers.
1880. Feb. 17.—682. Cave.
Apparatus for aerating, rousing, &c., malt liquors.
„ April 8.—1444. Barton.
Apparatus for mashing or brewing beer.

ATTEMPERATORS AND REFRIGERATORS.

1790. June 4.—1754. J. Long.
Utensils or methods to be employed in the essential parts of brewing good malt liquor, &c., &c.; and a means of cooling the tun.
„ July 28.—1769. T. Harris and J. Long.
Apparatus for use in breweries for the purpose of cooling worts of all kinds.
1801. May 2.—2495. H. Tickell.
Apparatus or refrigerator for cooling the worts or other fermented, fermentable, or dissolved animal or vegetable substances used in the process of brewing, or other manufacture of a similar nature.
1814. Feb. 14.—3778. J. Vallance.
Apparatus for cooling the worts, wash, &c., of brewers, vinegar-makers, and distillers.
1819. Jan. 15.—4331. R. Salmon and W. Warrell.
Cooling, condensing, and ventilating worts, liquors, and other fluids or solid matters—apparatus for the purpose.
1823. Nov. 1.—4858. W. Bundy.
Cooler for worts and wash. "Anti-evaporating cooler" to regulate the temperature of worts or wash in fermentation.
1826. May 23.—5368. D. P. Deurbrocq.
Apparatus for cooling wort or must previous to fermentation.
1827. July 18.—5526. R. Moore.
Preparing and cooling worts and wash from vegetable substances for the production of spirits.
1830. Aug. 5.—5974. Æ. Coffey.
Machinery used in brewing.
1849. Jan. 23.—12,439. R. Johnson.
Brewing—machinery connected with the process.
„ Mar. 28.—12,549. J. Lawrence.
Brewing worts for ale, porter, and other liquors.
1852. Mar. 8.—14,015. P. V. Kempen.
Refrigerator to be used in brewing and other similar purposes.
„ Oct. 19.—14,327. J. Palin and R. W. Seivier.
Brewing.
1853. Jan. 15.—106. H. C. Vion.
Apparatus for refrigerating.
1855. April 3.—737. E. T. Botta.
Method of, and apparatus for, beer brewing.
„ Nov. 15.—2577. G. Lister.
A cooling apparatus to be used in brewing.

1856. Jan. 30.—255. J. Gretton.
Brewing.
„ June 23.—1471. G. Riley.
An improved refrigerator for cooling brewers' and distillers' worts.
„ Nov. 28.—2814. O. Walker.
Brewing—machinery or apparatus employed therein.
1857. Jan. 21.—183. T. Harris.
Apparatus for refrigerating or cooling and regulating the temperature in worts and beer, which may also be employed as condensers in distilling.
„ „ 26.—227. W. L. Tizard.
Fermenting, cleansing, and attemperating apparatus to be employed in brewing.
„ Sept. 10.—2362. J. Harrison.
Apparatus for producing cold by the evaporation of volatile liquids in vacuo.
1858. May 6.—1011. J. Bridgman.
Improvements in cooling fluids, and in the application of cold.
„ June 15.—1353. W. P. Wilkins.
Arrangements and construction of refrigerating apparatus.
„ July 27.—1695. J. Long.
Cooling brewers' and distillers' worts and other liquids.
„ „ 30.—1718. J. Luis.
An apparatus for cooling beer and other liquids.
„ Oct. 15.—2303. T. Moore.
Refrigerators.
„ Dec. 7.—2802. J. J. Harriss.
Apparatus for refrigerating and regulating the temperature in worts and beer, which may also be employed as condensers in distilling.
1859. Jan. 10.—77. J. White.
Improvements in cleansing or purifying air, and in increasing or reducing the temperature thereof, and in the application of air so treated to sanitary and other uses.
„ Feb. 4.—320. R. A. Brooman.
Cooling worts and beer.
„ „ 12.—400. J. and J. Bennett.
Refrigerators for cooling beer and worts.
„ April 14.—935. J. Luis (Baudelot).
A new cooling apparatus for liquids, especially beer.
„ July 8.—1627. D. Mathews.
Apparatus for refrigerating and heating liquids.
„ Aug. 24.—1932. G. Riley.
Helical refrigerators for cooling brewers' and distillers' worts.
„ Sept. 17.—2118. J. Luis.
Cooling apparatus for liquids, especially beer.
„ „ 21.—2152. R. Davison.
Construction of holders for containing liquid or air, and other aeriform fluids, especially adapted for use in refrigerators.
„ Oct. 25.—2442. A. M'Glashan.
Refrigerators for cooling worts and other liquors.
„ „ 27.—2458. P. R. Hodge.
Improvements in the process of brewing fermented liquors, and in apparatus connected therewith, and in preparing and separating the materials, and the manner of using them in producing fermented liquors.

1859. Dec. 24.—2944. L. J. G. Rul.
An invention for preparing the dilution in distilleries and breweries by means of regularly heating and cooling instantaneously all the amylaceous, saccharine, fermentable substances.

1860. April 9.—887. H. Bridle.
Refrigerators.

„ May 21.—1246. W. Barker.
Improved apparatus for regulating the temperature of ale, beer, porter and other liquids during the process of fermentation.

„ June 4.—1368. C. Wateau.
An improved apparatus for cooling beer and other liquids.

„ July 4.—1614. G. S. Harris.
Apparatus for rapidly cooling or refrigerating water, wine, beer or other liquids.

„ Sept. 18.—2266. E. J. Hughes.
Brewing malt liquors—apparatus employed therein.

„ Oct. 15.—2503. G. Davies.
An improved method of, and apparatus for, refrigerating and freezing.

„ Nov. 29.—2934. J. A. Jaques, J. A. Fanshaw, and G. Jaques.
An improved mode of, and apparatus for, cooling liquids.

1861. Mar. 2.—534. T. Haigh and R. A. Robertson.
Apparatus applicable for boiling, cooling, and fermenting malt liquors, part of which may be applied to other purposes.

„ July 19.—1816. D. Gallafent.
Certain improvements in refrigerators for cooling liquids.

„ Sept. 30.—2435. J. Lush.
Mashing attemperators.

„ Dec. 7.—3069. R. Jolley.
An improved apparatus for heating, cooling, or drying, infusing, extracting, or absorbing vapours or gases for manufacturing, medical, or domestic purposes, and for preserving liquids and solids, alimentary or otherwise.

„ „ 18.—3179. C. Pontifex.
Refrigerators for cooling worts or other liquids.

1862. April 3.—939. R. Morton.
Improvements in refrigerators or apparatus for cooling liquids, parts of which improvements are also applicable to distillation, surface condensation, heating air for blast furnaces, and other similar purposes.

„ „ 29.—1256. W. L. Tizard.
Heating, cooling, and condensing apparatuses.

„ May 29.—1613. H. Boetius.
A new mode of cooling (refrigerating) hot liquids and condensing steam.

„ June 4.—1684. G. B. Toselli.
Apparatus for freezing and cooling liquids and mixing syrups.

„ Nov. 28.—3192. S. J. Browning.
Machines to be employed in brewing.

„ Dec. 30.—3470. J. Johnston.
An improved surface refrigerator.

1863. Aug. 3.—1916. H. Woods.
Apparatus used for regulating the temperatures during the process of fermentation in the union cask, tunning cask, or cleansing cask.

„ Sept. 16.—2270. J. Dannatt.
Construction of apparatus for cooling liquids.

1863. Oct. 26.—2646. A. Blake.
An improved refrigerator for cooling worts for brewing or other liquids requiring cooling, and for improving brewers' refrigerators now in use.

1864. April 8.—877. J. Picking.
Refrigerators or apparatus for refrigerating or cooling wort and other liquids.

„ Sept. 20.—2298. W. Lawrence.
Apparatus for mashing and cooling worts and other liquids.

„ Oct. 20.—2598. W. L. Tizard.
Improvements in brewing and distilling, and in apparatus employed therein, parts of which are applicable to the separation of liquids from solids.

„ Nov. 23.—2923. F. Millus.
An improved method of cooling liquids, particularly applicable to the cooling of wort.

1865. April 29.—1204. F. Gregory.
Machinery or apparatus employed in breweries and distilleries.

1866. Jan. 13.—115. N. W. Wheeler.
Means or apparatus for condensing steam and other vapours, and for refrigerating fluids.

„ „ 31.—302. J. Miller and J. Pyle.
Apparatus for cooling worts or other liquids.

„ Feb. 28.—615. H. A. Dufrené.
Improvements and new application in the manufacture of beer and alcoholic liquids.

„ Mar. 12.—747. G. Severn.
Improvements in the means and apparatus employed for evaporating and cooling liquids applicable to various purposes.

„ May 29.—1499. T. Haigh.
Coolers for the use of brewers and others.

„ „ 30.—1503. E..A. Pontifex.
Refrigerators.

„ June 6.—1560. W. Lawrence.
Manufacturers of, and apparatus for, the treatment of worts.

„ July 12.—1834. M. J. Roberts.
Cooling worts and other liquids.

„ Aug. 27.—2204. H. A. Dufrené.
Improvements in the manufacture of beer and other alcoholic liquids, and in the apparatus employed therefor.

„ Sept. 20.—2416. A. B. Walker.
Improvements in brewing, malting, distilling, and apparatus employed therein, parts of which are applicable for drying grain or other goods.

„ Oct. 1.—2526. A. M. Dix.
Refrigerators.

1867. Mar. 19.—787. F. Gregory.
Machinery or apparatus for refrigerating purposes used in breweries and distilleries.

„ „ 21.—817. H. Clifton.
Improvements in coolers for wine and other liquids and substances, and in vessels for protecting liquids and other substances from undesired effects of the atmosphere or atmospheric temperature, also in covers or stoppers for the same and other articles.

„ June 14.—1738. C. Askew.
Refrigerators for cooling worts and other liquids.

1867. June 15.—1751. A. M. Clark.
Improvements in the means of cooling beverages, also applicable for preserving substances from the action of heat.

„ July 6.—1988. G. Severn.
Refrigerators or apparatus for cooling worts and other liquids.

„ „ 11.—2031. J. Stirk and H. Bycroft.
Improvements in refrigerators for cooling worts and other liquids, which improvements are also applicable to condensers used in distillation.

„ Aug. 5.—2258. J. Dale.
A refrigerator for cooling worts.

„ „ 13.—2330. C. E. Flower.
Cooling brewers' worts and beer.

„ Sept. 26.—2707. J. Oxley.
Improvements in refrigerators for cooling worts and other liquids, which improvements are also applicable to condensers.

„ Oct. 19.—2944. J. Schwartz.
Cooling or refrigerating water.

1868. Feb. 4.—377. R. Morton.
Improvements in refrigerators or apparatus for cooling liquids, parts of which improvements are also applicable to distillation, surface condensation, and heating air for blast furnaces, or other purposes.

„ April 17.—1254. G. D. Kittoe and P. Brotherhood.
Improved apparatus for refrigerating or cooling worts and other liquids.

„ May 29.—1775. J. Neulleus and M. Neuhaus.
Portable apparatus for cooling wine or other liquids in bottles, or other like receptacles.

„ June 12.—1926. G. W. Cutmore.
Improvement in apparatus for cooling liquids in connecting pipes or tubes thereto, and in joining or connecting pipes for other purposes.

„ „ 13.—1937. W. Muller and G. Englert.
An improved apparatus for cooling beer and other malt liquids.

„ „ 17.—1965. G. B. Turrell.
Coolers for beer and other liquids.

„ July 31.—2408. G. D. Kittoe and P. Brotherhood.
Apparatus for cooling, heating, or tempering fluids.

„ Aug. 21.—2602. T. Haigh.
Apparatus to be used in brewing.

„ Oct. 26.—3278. W. Mort.
An improved method of, and apparatus for, obtaining reduction of temperature by the expansion of air or other permanent gases in special connection with the preservation of articles of food, the manufacture of ice, cooling of rooms and liquids.

„ Nov. 18.—3507. A. W. Drayson.
An improved mode of, and apparatus for, cooling wort and other liquids.

1869. June 1.—1694. J. A. Bindley.
An improved attemperator for union and tunning casks.

„ Oct. 6.—2906. E. A. Pontifex.
Refrigerator for cooling worts and other liquids.

„ Dec. 15.—3625. J. Askew.
A globular refrigerator for cooling brewers' worts.

1870. May 23.—1481. W. E. Heath.
Cooling or refrigerating beer, &c.

1870. Oct. 8.—2673. Frankenburg.
Apparatus for refrigerating liquids.
1871. Jan. 10.—54. Hydes and Bennett.
Cooling and condensing.
„ April 13.—975. Steel and Wilson.
Cooling worts.
„ „ 14.—992. Murdoch (Roettger).
Refrigerators.
„ May 3.—1189. Gamgee.
Producing cold.
„ „ 6.—1295. Gilbody (Reed).
Refrigerators, &c.
„ Sept. 2.—2324. Coles.
Cooling and refrigerating.
„ „ 28.—2563. Long.
Freezing and refrigerating.
„ „ 29.—2573. Coles.
Freezing and cooling.
„ Oct. 11.—2701. Murdoch (Roettger).
Refrigerating.
„ Nov. 10.—2898. Crane and McGraph.
Cooling and freezing.
„ Dec. 20.—3451. Purkis.
Refrigerating.
1872. Jan. 24.—228. Dufrené (Tellier).
Refrigerating.
„ Feb. 9.—420. Johnson (Gravenstine and Taylor).
Refrigerating.
„ April 22.—1203. Barlow (Naegile).
Cooling wort, &c.
„ June 26.—1935. Purkis.
Cooling liquids.
„ July 25.—2221. Phillips.
Cooling liquids.
„ Oct. 15.—3041. Steel.
Cooling liquids.
„ Dec. 9.—3732. Hill.
Refrigerating.
1873. Jan. 24.—290. Lake (Martin and Beath).
Cooling liquids.
„ Feb. 13.—536. Marsters.
Cooling liquids.
„ „ 27.—737. Marsters.
Cooling liquids.
„ Mar. 13.—935. Miller.
Cooling liquids, &c.
„ „ 24.—1083. Lawrence.
Cooling liquids, &c.
„ „ 25.—1106. Clark (Pasteur).
Brewing.
„ „ 28.—1158. West.
Refrigerating.
„ April 14.—1346. Barlow (Galland).
Refrigerating.
„ „ 21.—1443. Barlow (Galland).
Refrigerating.
„ June 19.—2153. Mort (Nicholl and Mort).
Refrigerating.

1873. July 5.—2332. Young (Ryle, jun.)
Refrigerating.
„ „ 16.—2460. Thomson.
Refrigerating.
„ „ 18.—2480. Thomas.
Refrigerating.
„ „ 21.—2500. Newbecker.
Cooling worts.
„ Oct. 28.—3495. Warren.
Refrigerators.
„ Nov. 29.—3902. Morton.
Refrigerators.
1874. Jan. 29.—383. Harrison.
Cooling worts, &c.
„ Feb. 23.—678. Barlow (Galland).
Cooling worts, &c.
„ Mar. 14.—936. Martin.
Cooling liquids, &c.
„ „ 21.—1001. Hacking.
Cooling liquids, &c.
„ April 30.—1523. Joyce (Selten).
Cooling worts.
„ May 21.—1801. Henderson and Ritchie.
Refrigerators.
„ Sept. 1.—2991. Bycrofts.
Refrigerating, &c.
1875. Jan. 29.—351. Weatherby.
Refrigerators for brewers.
„ Mar. 3.—775. Gooch.
Cooling liquids in breweries, &c.
„ April 26.—1530. Turnock.
Cooling wort, &c.
„ May 22.—1886. Walker.
Attemperating worts, &c.
„ July 3.—2413. Coughlin.
Cooling liquids.
„ „ 6.—2435. Severn.
Refrigerators for cooling wort.
„ Oct. 16.—3594. Pate (Cattell).
Producing air currents in refrigerators.
„ „ 25.—3699. Maw.
Cooling air for refrigerating.
„ Nov. 24.—4079. Barlow (Galland).
Cooling brewers' worts.
„ „ 10.—3907. Stanley.
Refrigerator.
1876. Jan. 5.—50. Franklin.
Cooling brewers' worts.
„ Feb. 17.—661. Ross.
Cooling breweries, &c.
„ „ „ —664. Walker.
Increasing cooling power of tubular refrigerator.
„ Aug. 1.—3076. Simpson.
Attemperating malt liquors, &c.
„ „ 31.—3427. Nishigawa and Hill.
Ice-making, cooling worts, &c.
„ Sept. 13.—3584. E. B. Smith.
Purifying and discharging air from refrigerators.

1876. Sept. 22.—3713. Lawrence.
Cooling wort, &c.
1877. Feb. 1.—437. Von Nawrocki (Schultz).
Compressed air machine for ice-making and supplying cold air to beer cellars, &c.
„ „ 6.—508. Henley.
Cooling or attemperating worts, &c., in brewing.
„ Mar. 12.—983. Hocking.
Annular tubular coolers, &c., for brewing.
„ „ 15.—1034. Bell and others.
Refrigerator for breweries.
„ „ 15.—1044. Pieper (Lipps).
Tubular cooling apparatus for breweries.
„ July 28.—2886. Wright.
Tubular apparatus for cooling worts.
„ Aug. 8.—3017. Southby.
Refrigerating brewers' worts.
„ Nov. 29.—4510. Walker.
Attemperating contents of "Burton unions."
1878. Feb. 12.—580. G. and W. Lawrence.
Corrugated refrigerator for cooling wort.
„ Mar. 8.—937. Young.
Refrigerator for cooling worts.
„ „ 21.—1122. Siddeley and McKay.
Cooling temperature of fermenting vessels.
„ May 23.—2078. Von Nawrocki (Littmann).
Cooling appliance for beer fermenting tubs.
„ July 26.—2972. Barnard (Cook).
Refrigerator for use in breweries.
„ Aug. 3.—3085. Harding.
Attemperator for wine, beer, &c.
„ „ 16.—3240. Brewer (Zsadamyi).
Cooling surfaces for cooling apparatus.
„ Sept. 10.—3579. Haddan (Pallauch).
Refrigerator for cooling beer.
„ Oct. 7.—3935. J. Harrison.
Wort cooling apparatus.
„ Nov. 23.—4777. Coleman.
Refrigerator for use in brewing.
„ Dec. 16.—5160. Lake (McMillan and Enright).
Pump for use in cooling air for preserving beer.
1879. Mar. 24.—1176. Lake (Pinto and Co.).
Refrigerating and freezing apparatus.
„ April 7.—1376. Johnson (Dalton and Co.).
Refrigerating and cooling apparatus.
„ May 24.—2080. Wise (Fanta).
Refrigerator for breweries.
„ „ 30.—2154. Miller and Durie.
Appliance for cooling, &c., liquids.
„ July 18.—2928. Latham and Way.
Improved means, &c., for regulating the temperature of liquids.
„ Aug. 25.—3418. Henderson and Low.
Implements for cooling warm liquids, &c.
„ Oct. 6.—4035. Wilson.
Apparatus for attemperating fluids, &c.
1880. Feb. 12.—621. Lake (Hunt and Pinto).
Refrigerating and freezing appliance.

1880. Feb. 17.—697. Hocking.
Refrigerating and cooling apparatus.
„ „ „ —703. Johnson (Savalle).
Refrigerating and condensing apparatus.
„ Mar. 19.—1188. Brice-Douglas.
Refrigerating apparatus.
„ May 17.—2010. Pieper (Windhausen).
Refrigerating and ice apparatus.

YEAST.

1787. Oct. 30.—1625. R. T. Blunt.
Making yeast for purposes of fermentation.
1803. June 21.—2715. P. Storck.
Substitute for brewers' yeast.
1812. Mar. 5.—3546. F. Mathew.
Manufacturing yeast.
1820. Nov. 1.—4506. H. L. Lobeck.
Manufacturing yeast.
1844. Dec. 20.—10,444. J. Thompson.
Preparation and application of various farinaceous products, machinery used in manufacturing same.
1849. Jan. 11.—12,411. M. Wrigley.
Making yeast or barm.
1856. Mar. 26.—728. W. E. Newton.
Macerating substances to be employed in the process of distillation.
„ Aug. 11.—1887. R. A. Brooman.
An improved fermenting agent.
„ Sept. 2.—2034. M. Aron.
An improved leaven.
„ „ 23.—2228. R. Winterbottom, jun.
Mode or method of making or producing dry barm or yeast.
„ Nov. 21.—2759. F. Ludewig.
An improved leaven.
1857. Jan. 26.—266. A. Hensel.
An invention for the manufacture of German yeast from flour.
„ „ 31.—286. A. Hensel.
Making compressed yeast.
1859. May 30.—1338. W. Clark.
A new manufacture of leaven.
„ Sept. 5.—2027. V. Tomell.
Manufacture of yeast.
1860. June 18.—1479. R. Dressel and A. Figge.
Manufacture of yeast.
1861. Sept. 3.—2196. P. Robertson.
Improvements in treating yeast.
1862. Feb. 25.—512. C. Kingsford.
A new composition for the manufacture of bread.
„ Mar. 1.—564. P. Robertson.
Improvements in treating yeast.
„ April 22.—1169. C. E. Elliott.
Preparation of dried yeast.
„ Nov. 10.—3032. W. E. Newton.
Treatment of maize or Indian corn preparatory to grinding the same into flour (and forming yeast).
1863. June 18.—1527. D. Barker.
Treatment and preservation of yeast.
1869. Jan. 25.—230. A. V. Newton.
An improvement in fermenting substances.

1869. Mar. 11.—741. J. B. Berrier.
An improvement for the preservation of yeast.
„ Aug. 25.—2530. G. Zoel and A. Lehmann.
A novel process of manufacturing yeast.
„ Oct. 2.—2867. A. Heathorn.
Preparation of yeast or barm.
1870. Feb. 8.—358. J. Ward and J. Bowing.
Preparing and drying yeast.
„ June 22.—1774. P. Boland.
An improved barm or yeast.
1873. Mar. 25.—1106. A. M. Clarke.
Improvements in the manufacture of beer and treatment of yeast.
1874. April 27.—1453. D. K. Clarke.
Improvements in machinery and apparatus for disintegrating and straining partially fluid or semi-solid substances.
„ May 26.—1846. J. H. Johnson.
Improvements in the manufacture of artificial yeast powder.
1877. Jan. 8.—80. Garrett.
Substitute for German or foreign yeast.
„ July 16.—2726. Liebert (Liebert).
Substitute for German yeast ("Alexandra yeast").
1878. Oct. 11.—4024. Garrett and Lederer.
Dry compound or substitute for brewers', &c., yeast.
„ „ 11.—4028. Hassell and Hehner.
Treating and preserving brewers' yeast.
„ Nov. 5.—4477. Griffin and Pearce.
Yeast sluice for fermenting backs.
„ „ 8.—4533. Von Nawrocki (Reichenkron).
Producing dry filiform yeast for preservation.
1879. Feb. 22.—722. Graham.
Treatment of brewers' yeast, whereby a powerful bakers' yeast is obtained.
„ Sept. 16.—3706. Handford (Marquart).
Manufacture of yeast.
„ Dec. 13.—5106. Haig.
Manufacture of yeast.
1880. Feb. 21.—778. Lake (Rainer).
Manufacture of yeast.

HOP AND YEAST PRESSES.

1796. Feb. 22.—2091. F. Mathew.
Separating beer from the yeast; preserving yeast in any climate.
1832. Sept. 29.—6316. J. Swan.
Brewing.
1837. Mar. 21.—7328. M. Poole.
Making fermented liquors.
„ April 18.—7347. C. Farina.
Obtaining fermentable matter from grain; manufacturing the same for various purposes.
1838. Oct. 11.—7829. M. Heath.
Clarifying and filtering beer, wine, and other liquids.
1852. Oct. 25.—513. S. Plimsoll.
Thoroughly and effectually cleansing, extracting, or fining ale, beer, porter, and other malt liquors from the yeast bottoms, barm, &c.
1853. April 27.—1009. Do. do. do.
1854. Aug. 25.—1864. R. B. Froggart.
Method of clarifying fermented liquids, machinery, or apparatus used in the said process.

1855. April 3.—750. Mr. Evrard.
An improved continuous drawing-compressor for moulding or bruising several substances or mixtures.

1859. Jan. 1.—15. A. Prince.
Construction of cylindrical press.

„ Feb. 1.—290. G. A. Waller.
Means of, and apparatus for, expressing liquid from semi-fluid substances, and other substances containing liquid.

„ July 28.—1756. P. Robertson.
Manufacture of beer, ale, porter, and spirits.

„ Sept. 3.—2013. H. R. L. Schramm.
A new process for pressing and separating simultaneously the fibres and pellicles contained in the constituent matters of beer grains, &c.

1860. May 9.—1142. R. Geoghegan.
Machinery or apparatus for expressing liquids from various substances.

„ June 7.—1408. G. A. Waller.
Apparatus for filtering and solidifying.

„ Sept. 25.—2331. R. Geoghegan.
Machinery or apparatus for expressing liquids from various substances.

1861. Dec. 24.—3217. J. Rosindell.
An improved method of, and apparatus for, separating solid from liquid substances.

1862. June 13.—1762. J. Ives.
Improved apparatus for expressing juice from fruit and other vegetable substances.

„ „ 16.—1780. G. H. Birkbeck.
Construction of presses for extracting liquids from various substances.

„ Sept. 10.—2491. G. Ritchie.
Improvements in extracting the liquid portion of yeast, spent hops, or other similar matters, and in the apparatus employed therein.

„ „ 23.—2594. C. Pontifex.
Means or apparatus for removing or expressing beer from yeast or from hops.

„ Oct. 7.—2706. J. Oxley.
Apparatus for expressing and separating beer from yeast or barm.

„ „ 30.—2927. F. Gregory.
Presses for pressing seeds, fruits, hops, and other substances.

1863. July 4.—1670. J. Oxley.
Filtering apparatus.

„ Oct. 5.—2439. R. Pepper.
An improved machine for pressing or crushing spent hops.

1864. Jan. 29.—250. T. M. Heathorn.
Machinery for separating liquid from solid substances containing liquid.

„ Mar. 19.—701. J. B. Jude.
Presses or apparatus to be employed for pressing yeast, and for other similar purposes.

„ April 23.—1024. G. J. Worssam.
Machinery and apparatus for expressing liquids or moisture from substances.

„ Oct. 20.—2598. W. L. Tizard.
Improvements in brewing and distilling, and in apparatus employed therein, parts of which are applicable to the separation of liquids from solids.

1865. April 29.—1204. F. Gregory.
Machinery or apparatus employed in breweries and distilleries.

1867. Feb. 6.—330. G. A. Waller.
Constructing and working apparatus for filtering beer and other liquids.

„ Sept. 7.—2540. H. Woods.
Presses for extracting liquid from hops, seeds, and other substance.

„ „ 20.—2652. W. Hall.
Improvements in separating yeast from liquid matters, and in apparatus to be used therefor.

„ Dec. 12.—3503. C. Kerby.
Improved apparatus for filtering liquids.

1868. Jan. 8.—72. C. Pontifex.
Presses or apparatus for expressing worts from spent hops, the same being applicable for expressing fluids from other matters.

„ May 18.—1624. W. Needham and J. Kite.
Preparing filtering surfaces for the depuration of fluids.

1870. Feb. 10.—389. C. and F. Pontifex, and A. Sherwood.
Improvements in machinery or apparatus for pressing hops.

1875. May 14.—1806. H. T. Brown.
An improved method of recovering the brewers' wort.

1877. June 28.—2502. J. E. Bennett.
Expressing liquids from spent hops.

1878. May 22.—2043. Freakley.
Press or machine for filtering hops.

„ Oct. 3.—3896. Gretton.
Machine for treating spent hops.

1879. July 31.—3104. Siddeley and Dearn.
Apparatus for extracting moisture from hops and yeast.

BOILING.

1692. June 28.—299. J. Tatham.
Small copper boiler and wooden vessel for brewing and distilling liquors and spirits.

1720. June 25.—430. J. T. Desaguliers, D. Niblet, and W. Vreein.
Making the steam of boiling liquor useful for drying malt and hops.

1736. Nov. 15.—555. J. Payne.
Boilers for brewing and distilling.

1773. Nov. 17.—1056. C. Chrisel.
Constructing and setting boilers for brewhouses and distilleries.

1784. Nov. 17.—1445. S. T. Wood.
Constructing and adapting coppers, boilers, tubes, and other hollow bodies for heating water and worts, rendering the same air-tight.

1787. Feb. 3.—1590. J. Reinecke.
Machine to be used in all household purposes where boiling is required, applicable also in the operations of boiling in manufactories.

1788. Nov. 6.—1673. J. Rumsey.
Constructing boilers for distillation and for other objects.

1789. June 9.—1685. M. Howson.
Boilers for distilling.

1790. June 4.—1754. J. Long.
Utensils or methods to be employed in the essential parts of brewing good malt liquors, &c.

1791. Sept. 12.—1826. R. Hare.
Apparatus for preserving and applying the essential oil of hops, and for heating water for brewing without the application of fire.

1809. June 8.—8240. J. F. Archbold.
Brewing.

1811. Sept. 23.—3493. J. Needham.
Portable apparatus for brewing beer and ale from malt.

1812. June 9.—3575. J. Needham.
Portable apparatus for brewing beer from malt and hops.

1813. Sept. 4.—3737. F. Parkinson.
Boiler for distilling to preserve spirits and other articles from waste in distilling and boiling.

1815. June 1.—3920. J. Kilby.
Brewing malt liquors.

1837. April 18.—7347. C. Farina.
Obtaining fermentable matter from grain, manufacturing the same for various purposes.

1841. April 5.—8919. J. Beilby.
Brewing.

1846. June 29.—11,268. J. Moreland.
Setting and fixing coppers, stills, and boilers.

1847. Feb. 20.—11,586. J. C. Robertson.
Distilling application of the materials used therein, and suitable thereto to other manufacturing purposes.

1848. Nov. 29.—12,344. J. Lane and J. Taylor.
Brewing.

1852. Oct. 19.—14,327. J. Palin and R. W. Siever.
Brewing.

1853. June 3.—1363. F. L. Gossart.
A system of permanent circulation of caloric, intended to produce and overheat steam, gas, and liquids.

„ Sept. 24.—2207. C. Maitland and W. Gorrie.
Apparatus for heating water and other liquids.

„ Oct. 4.—2268. D. T. Shears.
Improvements in brewing.

1854. Mar. 20.—663. J. Young.
Brewing.

1855. April 3.—737. F. T. Botta.
Method of, and apparatus for, beer brewing.

1857. April 11.—1026. W. G. Wiles.
Brewing.

1858. May 13.—1079. A. M. Dix.
Certain improvements in the process of brewing or obtaining decoctions, and in apparatus connected therewith, which apparatus is also applicable to condensing, refrigerating, or other such like purposes.

„ July 8.—1536. P. R. Hodge.
Brewing fermented liquors, treating materials used therein for purposes of food.

„ Aug. 3.—1759. J. Steel.
Brewing and distilling.

„ Nov. 19.—2613. G. Howie and J. Norton.
An improved method of boiling water or worts for breweries, &c., by steam.

1859. Oct. 8.—2294. P. Robertson.
Repairing, boiling, and fermenting worts, maturing beer, spirits, and cider.

1859. Dec. 24.—2944. L. J. G. Rul.
An invention for preparing the dilution in the distilleries and breweries by means of regularly heating and cooling instantaneously all the amylaceous, saccharine, fermented substances.

1860. Feb. 22.—478. R. Davison.
Boiling worts and other liquids.

„ Nov. 15.—2799. J. Matthews.
Brewing.

1861. Jan. 2.—11. E. B. West.
Improvements in the processes of making worts and washes in brewing and distilling, and in combination and adaptation of apparatus connected with the same, and for novel apparatus connected with the same.

„ Feb. 1.—273. H. Medlock.
Brewing malt liquors.

1862. April 26.—1256. W. L. Tizard.
Heating, cooling, and condensing apparatus.

„ Aug. 30.—2408. F. Le Conte.
Construction of furnaces for steam boilers used in sugar mills, distilleries, breweries, and other mills.

1863. May 28.—1345. T. Jarvis.
Improvements in obtaining vegetable extracts, and in apparatus employed therein.

„ Sept. 19.—2312. J. C. Pooley.
Brewing or preparing beverages from malt and hops.

„ Dec. 2.—3032. R. L. Clifton.
Apparatus used for brewing.

1864. Jan. 14.—101. W. J. Murphy.
An improved steam brewing copper.

1866. May 17.—1398. J. Hampton.
Furnaces for obtaining perfect consumption of fuel.

„ Oct. 24.—2744. J. Watts.
Improvements in furnaces and fire-places, and in utilizing the waste heat of the said furnaces (heating malt kilns).

1867. Oct. 1.—2760. G. Allibon and A. Manbré.
Improvements in apparatus applicable to the conversion of cereal and vegetable substances into saccharine matter, in treating substances extracted from malt, fruits, &c.

1868. Mar. 30.—1082. A. B. Walker.
Improvements in the application of hot blast or heated air for evaporating salt brine and other liquids; raising steam in boilers; boiling worts, &c.

„ Sept. 23.—2930. H. Woods.
Apparatus for heating water by means of steam.

1869. Jan. 8.—64. J. Rodgers.
Furnace for brewing pans, &c.

„ Mar. 11.—746. J. Waddington, jun., A. Waddington, and F. Bell.
A new or improved method for condensing and utilizing steam or other vapour arising from the boiling of liquids, worts, &c.

„ Sept. 20.—2735. W. A. Gilbee.
Improvements in apparatus for heating wines and other fermentable liquids.

„ Oct. 28.—2842. J. Rennie and T. Halliday.
Furnaces for boiling worts.

1871. Feb. 28.—541. J. Rennie.
Improvements in furnaces.

„ April 12.—962. T. Halliday.
Improvements in brewers' furnaces.

1871. May 23.—1381. T. H. Granger and J. P. L. Hyan.
Improvements in means to heat worms.
„ Aug. 31.—2290. J. Leadbetter.
Improvements in apparatus to be used for brewing.
„ Nov. 9.—3026. R. Willison.
Improvements in apparatus for heating.
1872. July 29.—2257. A. Moore and J. Watt.
An improved apparatus for heating liquids.
„ Aug. 7.—2351. G. M. Moore.
Improvements in the process of evaporating.
„ „ 12.—2395. J. G. Williams.
Improvements in apparatus for heating liquids.
1873. June 7.—2028. T. Beans.
An improved apparatus for boiling liquor.
„ Sept. 15.—3018. E. Marsden.
Improvements in pans for boiling down.
1874. Feb. 23.—678. H. B. Barlow.
Improvements in brewing and machinery therein.
1875. May 22.—1886. A. B. Walker.
Improvements in machinery, plant, &c.
1876. Feb. 17.—664. A. B. Walker.
Improvements in apparatus for heating, &c.
„ Sept. 8.—3539. Murdoch (Kirkpatrick).
Evaporating wort.
1877. Nov. 9.—4194. Steel.
Vessels or copper for boiling worts.
„ Dec. 18.—4808. Wilson.
Arranging apparatus in copper to avoid striking out of hops after each boiling.
1878. Mar. 21.—1121. Fenwick.
Boiling pan and furnace for brewers.
„ Oct. 26.—4305. Barraclough.
Combined steam and water pipe apparatus for heating and supplying water for brewing.
1880. Jan. 22.—277. Moss and Wright.
Vessels for boiling brewers' worts.
„ May 13.—1967. Wilson.
Improvement in the process of boiling worts, &c.

FERMENTING.

1790. June 6.—1754. J. Long.
Utensils or methods to be employed in the essential parts of brewing good malt liquors, &c.
1798. June 19.—2245. R. Shannon and R. Burnett.
Process of fermentation, brewing utensils, and pneumatic apparatus for the purpose.
1807. Mar. 7.—3017. J. F. Atlee.
Apparatus to be used in fermenting liquors.
1830. July 19.—5959. E. Riley.
Process and apparatus for fermenting malt and other liquors.
1834. June 7.—6623. E. Keele.
Valve and apparatus for close fermenting and cleansing porter, beer, and ale.
1838. May 31.—7658. P. Walker.
Apparatus to be used in cleansing beer, or other fermented liquors.
1841. April 5.—8921. W. L. Tizard.
Apparatus for brewing.

1847. Feb. 20.—11,586. J. C. Robertson.
Brewing—application of the materials used therein to other manufacturing purposes.
1848. Nov. 29.—12,344. J. Lane and J. Taylor.
Brewing.
1849. Jan. 29.—12,439. R. Johnson.
Brewing—machinery connected with the process.
1852. Oct. 19.—14,327. J. Palin and R. W. Seiver.
Brewing.
„ Dec. 3.—942. P. and R. B. Walker.
Fermenting ale and porter, and other liquids.
1854. June 27.—1413. C. H. Collette.
Manufacture of beer.
„ July 26.—1647. W. L. Tizard.
Fermentation—apparatus employed therein.
„ Sept. 8.—1957. J. Youill.
Fermenting liquors—machinery or apparatus employed therein.
1856. June 14.—1407. H. Mege.
Manufacture of bread (fermenting).
„ Nov. 22.—2775. R. A. Brooman.
Manufacture of artificial wines, or beverages to be substituted for wines, apparatus for aiding fermentation.
1857. Jan. 26.—227. W. L. Tizard.
Fermenting, cleansing, and attemperating apparatus to be employed in brewing.
„ June 29.—1818. J. Lawrence.
Apparatus for brewing.
1858. Nov. 3.—2453. V. Blumberg.
Improvements in the construction of slate billiard tables, which improvements are also applicable for other useful purposes (vats).
1859. Feb. 9.—371. E. Herring.
Mashing and fermenting of grain for the production of alcohol.
„ Oct. 8.—2294. P. Robertson.
Repairing, boiling, and fermenting worts.
1860. Sept. 1.—2120. G. Hollands.
Improved apparatus to be used in the process of fermentation.
1861. Mar. 7.—583. G. Hollands.
Mode of, and apparatus used in the process of, fermentation.
„ „ 14.—638. E. A. Pontifex.
Charging, tunning, or fermenting casks and vessels.
„ June 29.—1662. A. Wood.
Construction of fermenting-tuns and apparatus for storing beer.
„ July 24.—1858. A. Wood.
Apparatus employed for fermenting purposes in brewing beer, as also for storing beer and for general purposes of fermentation.
1863. Feb. 28.—567. J. Maxfield.
Certain improvements in brewing and in apparatus employed therein.
„ Sept. 12.—2247. J. King.
Improved means for assisting and regulating the process of fermentation.
1864. Mar. 1.—507. W. H. Mellor.
An improved apparatus to be used when fermenting malt liquors in casks or other like close vessels.
„ Sept. 12.—2222. J. Williams.
Apparatus connected with fermenting, charging, cleansing, or tunning vessels, casks, or vats.

1864. Sept. 29.—2394. J. Watts.
Apparatus to be used in the fermentation of wort and other fermentable liquids.

„ Oct. 14.—2535. J. Watts.
Apparatus for conducting the fermentation of wort and other fermentable liquids.

„ „ 20.—2598. W. L. Tizard.
Improvements in brewing and distilling, and in apparatus employed therein, parts of which are applicable to the separation of liquids from solids.

„ Nov. 3.—2719. C. Garton.
Brewing, fermenting, racking, and bottling beer, ale, and wine.

1866. June 6.—1560. W. Lawrence.
Manufacture of, and apparatus for, treatment of worts.

1871. May 24.—1390. J. W. Smith.
Improvements in the method of fermenting worts.

1872. Aug. 12.—2395. J. G. Williams.
Improvements in apparatus for fermenting liquids.

„ Nov. 19.—3449. R. Davison.
Improvements in brewing apparatus.

1873. May 5.—1612. S. S. Lees and F. Faulkener.
Improvements in rousing apparatus.

„ June 17.—2129. E. Beans.
Improvements in brewing and treating fermented liquors.

„ Dec. 22.—4203. W. Hodson.
Improvements in apparatus for cleansing casks.

1874. April 29.—1488. T. B. Pye.
Improved arrangement or apparatus for feeding liquors to fermenting vessels.

„ May 19.—1768. J. Hartley.
Certain improvements in the construction of fermenting vats.

1875. Feb. 18.—601. W. Cutler.
Improvements in the construction of fermenting squares.

„ May 22.—1886. A. B. Walker.
Improvements in machinery, &c., for breweries.

„ „ 24.—1894. E. Savill.
Improvements in apparatus for skimming.

„ Nov. 24.—4079. H. B. Barlow.
Improvements in the fermentation of beer.

1876. Sept. 7.—3521. H. Boddington.
Method of, and apparatus for, rousing fermenting liquors.

„ Nov. 25.—4573. Rands.
Adding phosphate of ammonia to wort, &c., for fermenting same.

1877. July 30.—2896. Simmons.
Aerating beer or wort during fermentation.

1878. May 23.—2052. Graham.
Filtering and using air in fermenting worts.

„ July 24.—2954. Orchart and Walpole.
Vessel for applying to casks, &c., to receive overflow from fermentation.

BREWING.

1636. Mar. 26.—90. Sir W. Bromicker.
Drawing double the quantity of aqua vitæ from a given quantity of liquor, also extracting a larger quantity of strong water from malt than has hitherto been usual.

1788. Mar. 4.—1641. W. Ker.
Brewing ale, beer, porter, and other malt liquors.

1790. June 4.—1754. J. Long.
Utensils or methods to be employed in the essential parts of brewing good malt liquor.
1798. Feb. 1.—2212. R. Shannon.
Process of distilling.
1807. Sept. 9.—3072. J. Day.
Compounding Dantzic spruce or black beer.
1809. Sept. 26.—3263. R. J. de Roche.
Brewing.
1813. Feb. 20.—3651. J. Roberts.
Concentrating or reducing such parts of malt and hops as are requisite in making ale, beer, and porter.
1825. Feb. 10.—5091. G. A. Lamb.
Composition of malt and hops.
1839. Mar. 26.—8013. H. M. Grover.
Brewing by use of a material not hitherto so used.
1845. April 29.—10,641. W. Maughan and A. Dunlop, jun.
Manufacture of ale, porter, and other fermented liquors.
„ Nov. 27.—10,973. W. Maughan and A. Dunlop, jun.
Manufacture of ale, porter, and other fermented liquors.
1847. Feb. 20.—11,586. J. C. Robertson.
Brewing—application of the materials used therein to other manufacturing purposes.
1851. April 2.—13,582. T. Huckvale.
Treating mangel-wurzel, and making drinks and other preparations therefrom.
1852. Oct. 19.—14,327. J. Palin and R. W. Seiver.
Brewing.
1853. Mar. 2.—522. E. D. Moore.
Mode of treating the extract of malt and hops.
„ May 14.—1196. H. D. Mertens.
Preparing materials to be employed in making beer and other beverages.
1854. July 10.—1509. D. Beck.
Brewing and distilling.
„ Nov. 6.—2341. W. Collis.
Brewing.
1856. Nov. 7.—2619. H. Dircks.
Preparation and application of the materials for making worts and washes, in brewing, distilling, and like operations; apparatus connected with the same.
„ „ 28.—2814. P. Walker.
Brewing machinery or apparatus employed therein.
1857. Sept. 21.—2448. E. B. West.
Improvements in the manner of preparing and applying materials used in brewing to that purpose, and in the various processes and apparatus used in connection with the same, and for novel apparatus connected with the same.
„ Nov. 7.—2822. J. Fordred.
Treating and purifying water.
1858. June 5.—1271. A. Manbré.
An improved method of preparing malt and other grain, and in extracting the saccharine matter therefrom, whether for the purpose of brewing, distilling, or otherwise.
„ „ 7.—1283. J. B. A. Lombard and A. T. Esquiron.
A new or improved method of obtaining saccharine substances from cereal and vegetable matters, and applying the products obtained to various useful purposes.

1860. Feb. 4.—298. P. Robertson.
Improvements in brewing beer, ale, and porter; also in separating brewers' worts from grain and beer, ale and porter, from yeast and other matters, and also in apparatus used for these and like purposes.

„ „ 24.—510. C. Wetter.
Manufacture of fermented and spirituous liquors.

„ April 3.—859. A. N. Jensen.
Improvements in brewing worts from saccharine and farinaceous substances, with a new method of retaining the aroma.

„ Oct. 6.—2424. A. Sarjeant.
Malt liquors.

1861. Mar. 28.—775. L. J. Vandecasteele.
Brewing.

„ May 30.—1353. A. Blake.
Improvements in the process of brewing.

1862. April 10.—1028. G. D. Mertens.
Improvements in the preparation of materials to be employed in the making of beer, and in the machinery or apparatus employed therein.

„ Aug. 23.—2360. E. W. Newton.
Mode of, and apparatus for, treating fermentable substances for brewing and distilling.

1864. July 8.—1695. A. Blake.
Improving water for the purposes of brewing, and beer produced therefrom.

1865. July 6.—1781. T. S. Prideaux.
Improving draught beer, ale, porter, and cider.

1866. Aug. 30.—2241. H. E. Newton.
An improved process for treating and preserving beer and other fermented liquors.

„ Sept. 7.—2298. J. Schneider.
A process of making improved beer and ale.

1867. July 22.—2137. W. E. Newton.
Improvements in brewing, and in apparatus employed therein.

„ Nov. 27.—3359. E. Belknap.
Treatment of the solution of malt for brewing.

1868. Mar. 13.—861. Mr. Rowand.
Treatment or preparation of the ingredients employed in the manufacture of fermented liquors.

„ Oct. 8.—3081. J. Steel.
Apparatus for obtaining extracts from roasted malt.

1869. April 12.—1121. E. Beaues.
Brewing (use of magnesium, &c.).

„ Dec. 31.—3785. F. J. Bolton.
Treatment of fermented liquors.

1870. Mar. 26.—895. W. Bailey.
Brewing fermented liquors.

„ May 10.—1336. W. R. Lake.
Process of brewing ale, &c.

„ Aug. 11.—2231. S. Bennett.
Improvements in preparation of worts.

1871. Aug. 7.—2082. J. H. Johnson.
Improvements in manufacture of beer.

„ „ 10.—2101. C. P. Matthews.
Improvements in brewing beers and other liquors.

„ „ 24.—2225. L. Pasteur.
Improvements in brewing.

1872. Mar. 25.—889. W. Garton.
Improvements in brewing.
„ April 5.—1031. F. Coates.
An improvement in the manufacture of beer.
1874. Dec. 15.—4312. W. T. Read.
Improvements in the preservation of fermented liquors.
1876. Nov. 30.—4649. Nicholls.
Save-all for ale cask to receive workings.
1877. Jan. 2.—27. Lake (Heusner).
Beer testing apparatus.
„ Mar. 26.—1183. Lockwood.
Treating and hopping beer, &c.
„ Dec. 10.—4693. Hancock.
Preserving and recovering sour beer.
1878. April 20.—1611. Renard and Haye.
Pneumatic elevator for use in breweries.
„ June 10.—2321. Sezille.
Treating raw maize for making beer.
„ July 20.—2897. Perrot.
Product for preserving beer.
„ Aug. 24.—3334. Atkins.
Compound gases for de-alcoholizing beer.
„ Oct. 19.—4170. Copley.
Rendering water permanently hard for use in brewing.
„ Nov. 8.—4533. Von Nawrocki (Reichenkron).
Producing concentrated beer wort for preservation, yeast for fermenting same.
1879. Mar. 14.—1025. Wirth (Holderer).
Manufacture of beer.
„ „ 17.—1051. Farquhar.
Appliance for separating beer from the "grounds," &c.
„ June 27.—2590. Welz and Rittner.
Method, &c., of brewing.
„ July 11.—2834. Kunkler.
Concentrating beer, &c.
„ Aug. 16.—3305. Collingridge & Co.
Auxiliary apparatus for brewing.
„ Sept. 5.—3573. Rickaby.
Apparatus for heating, &c., water for brewing.
„ Oct. 29.—4420. A. O. Stopes.
Brewers' finings.
„ Nov. 27.—4848. Tillmann.
Preparing wort, &c.
„ Dec. 1.—4910. Engel (Ross).
Treatment of beer, &c.
„ „ 10.—5060. Munns.
Apparatus for improving condition of beer.
1880. Feb. 5.—512. McGaan.
Manufacture of fermented liquors.
„ „ 14.—655. Collingridge and Lecerf.
Improvements in method of brewing, &c.
„ „ 16.—669. Atkins.
Appliance for preserving beer.
„ „ 17.—704. Daniel.
Treatment of worts, &c.
„ April 10.—1471. Gillman and Spencer.
Preserving beer and recovering when sour.

1880. May 13.—1972. Mèrichenski.
Apparatus for raising malt liquors.
„ „ 20.—2061. Lovett.
Apparatus for indicating the height and showing the condition of the beer in casks, &c.

FILTERS.

1877. Feb. 10.—567. Bowing.
Filter press for treating beers.
„ Mar. 2.—847. Greger.
Applying air filter to vent pegs.
„ Aug. 8.—3019. Bonnefin.
Filter press.
„ „ 27.—3253. Derbyshire.
Filter press and bags for same.
„ Sept. 3.—3349. Rohde.
Air filter for beer pumps.
„ „ 18.—3515. Kemp-Welsh.
Filter press.
1878. Jan. 30.—289. J. Hodson.
Passing beer through a filter of dry hops.
„ Mar. 21.—1132. Rawlings.
Filter press.
„ May 22.—2403. Freakley.
Filter press.
„ Aug. 9.—3147. Bell.
Filter press for saccharine liquors.
„ Dec. 10.—5051. Wegelin and Hübner.
Filter press for beer.
1879. May 10.—1869. Scott and Ogilvie.
Purifying saccharine substances.
„ „ 28.—2120. Thomson (Belcher).
Filtering saccharine solutions.
„ Nov. 1.—4461. Alsing.
Filter press.
1880. Jan. 5.—38. Johnson.
Filter press.
„ Feb. 10.—623. Elmore.
Device for intercepting hops, &c., in ales, &c.

KILNS.

1876. Sept. 26.—3749. Perry.
Malting kiln for drying malt.
„ Nov. 6.—4713. Johnson (Völckner).
Mechanical pneumatic malting apparatus.
1878. Jan. 1.—9. Hildebrandt (Hahn).
Tower-formed mechanical malt kiln.
„ Dec. 4.—4958. Lake (Boynton).
Kiln for drying malt, grain, &c.

SUGAR, GLUCOSE, SACCHARINE, Etc.

1876. Nov. 25.—4573. Rands.
Treating sugar for brewing with ammonia phosphate.
„ Dec. 26.—4995. Lake (Boomer and Randall).
Malt syrup or extract.

1877. Jan. 15.—190. Johnson (Bernard and Ehrmann).
Using magnesia for defecating saccharine juices, reviving same.
„ April 11.—1405. Jackson and Mellor.
Concentrating saccharine solutions.
„ May 19.—1968. Clark (Chiozza).
Treating maize for making glucose.
„ June 9.—2251. Pitt (Smith and others).
Using glycerine for evaporating saccharine juices.
„ Aug. 16.—3117. Irwin.
Utilizing glucose refuse in making cattle food.
„ Dec. 8.—4672. Johnson (Seyferth).
Obtaining saccharine solutions from purified saccharate of lime.
1878. Feb. 4.—456. Johnson.
Treating maize, &c., to produce glucose.
„ Oct. 26.—4301. Simon (Kühnemann).
Treating seeds for extracting glucose for use in brewing.
1879. April 16.—1484. Gill (Sutton).
Evaporating saccharine and other liquids.
„ May 10.—1869. Scott and Ogilvie.
Purifying saccharine substances.
„ June 23.—2502. Beanes.
Manufacture of glucose.
„ Nov. 26.—4831. Johnson (Weinrich).
Treatment of saccharine.
1880. Jan. 21.—268. Clark (Dangiville).
Improvements for obtaining glucose and alcohol.
„ Mar. 13.—1088. Harvey.
Treatment of saccharine juices for concentrating same.

SUNDRIES.

1632. July 20.—59. T. Gent.
Waterwork instrument, or a corrected crane for passing wine, oil, or other liquor from one vessel to another without sinking or forcing by the mouth.
1797. Oct. 31.—2196. J. Bramah.
Retaining, clarifying, and drawing off malt and other liquors.
1798. Aug. 7.—2257. T. Staton.
Apparatus for raising beer, ale, wine, spirits, oil, or other liquids from cellars or other low places to a more elevated situation.
„ Dec. 17.—2280. W. Hart.
Apparatus for raising beer, ale, &c., from the cellar to the bar or other part of the house.
1800. Feb. 1.—2369. T. Parkinson.
Hydrostatic machine for drawing beer or other liquids out of a cellar or vaults.
1802. Nov. 6.—2656. T. Barnett.
Invention whereby a requisite quantity of air would introduce itself into any vessel containing fluid, so as to preserve the fluid, and prevent it being flat.
1810. Mar. 22.—3320. J. Gregory.
Tunning ale and beer in casks; cleansing ales and beers.
1825. Feb. 19.—5097. T. Masterman.
Apparatus for bottling wine, beer, and other liquids with increased economy and despatch.
1830. Mar. 30.—5924. W. Aitken.
Keeping or preserving beer, ale, and other fermented liquors (injecting carbonic gas).

1834. July 17.—6647. J. Warne.
Machinery for raising, drawing, or forcing beer, ale, and other liquids or fluids.

1836. July 14.—7152. C. Phillips.
Drawing off beer and other liquids from casks or vessels.

1837. April 4.—7336. W. Wynn.
Apparatus for diminishing the evaporation of vinous, alcoholic, acetous, and other volatile vapours, and preventing the absorption of noxious effluvia in vinous and other fluids.

1838. Feb. 24.—7574. M. Poole.
Preserving wine and other fermented liquids in bottles.

„ Dec. 6.—7899. M. Berry.
Filling bottles with gaseous liquids; retaining or emptying them.

1839. Sept. 11.—8216. S. Stocker.
Beer, cider, and spirit engines.

1840. Mar. 7.—8421. H. Taylor.
Apparatus for filling and closing bottles.

„ May 13.—8511. H. Ernest.
Manufacture of beer engines.

„ Aug. 3.—8588. G. E. Noone.
Engines for drawing beer, cider, and other fluids.

1841. April 5.—8921. W. L. Tizard.
Apparatus for brewing.

1843. April 20.—9708. J. M'Innes.
Funnels for conducting liquids into vessels.

„ „ 25.—9740. S. Beadon.
Apparatus for regulating the inclination of vessels for drawing off liquids contained therein; means of drawing off liquids.

„ Oct. 27.—9917. A. G. Hull.
Manufacturing fermented and distilled liquors (passing a current of electricity through the liquor).

1844. July 30.—10,279. T. Warne.
Engines for raising, forcing, and drawing beer, ale, or other liquids.

1845. April 10.—10,608. S. Stocker.
Machinery for lifting, forcing, or conveying liquids into vessels for holding the same.

„ June 3.—10,698. M. Poole.
Drawing off liquids impregnated with gases from vessels containing the same, and closing such vessels.

„ Nov. 20.—10,967. J. Depledge.
Metallic broacher.

„ Dec. 12.—11,003. M. Poole.
Filling bottles and other vessels.

1846. April 28.—11,179. S. Pickford.
Apparatus for raising or forcing ale, and other fermented liquors, for draught.

„ May 13.—11,206. C. Vaux.
Apparatus employed when transmitting and drawing beer and ale.

„ „ 26.—11,223. W. Mayo.
Bottling aerated and other liquids.

„ Dec. 1.—11,471. W. Mayo.
Apparatus used when pumping liquids; also bottling fluids.

1847. Feb. 8.—11,563. C. Vaux.
Storing and supplying beer, ale, and porter.

„ Mar. 2.—11,604. A. Crosse.
Treating fermentable and other liquids, so as to cause impurities or matters to be extracted or precipitated.

1848. Jan. 11.—12,019. A. Ade, R. Hely, and J. E. Norton.
Mode of machinery for filling bottles and vessels.

„ May 22.—12,159. G. H. Bursill, J. Paterson, and J. Matthews.
Treating malt liquors, and other liquids or fluids; machinery for effecting such treatment.

„ July 29.—12,227. R. Abbey.
Preserving fermented and other liquids, and matters in vessels.

„ Aug. 21.—12,250. J. Bethell.
Preserving animal and vegetable substances from decay.

„ Nov. 18.—12,330. T. Masters.
Apparatus for charging bottles and other vessels with gaseous fluid; also for drawing off fluids.

1849. Mar. 28.—12,549. J. Lawrence.
Storing ale, porter, and other liquors.

„ June 20.—12,665. R. A. Brooman.
Apparatus for transferring liquids from one vessel to another, and for filling bottles and other vessels with liquids.

„ Nov. 17.—12,852. S. Stocker.
Beer engines.

1850. May 8.—13,074. J. Youill.
Machine or apparatus for washing, cleansing, filling, and corking bottles and other vessels.

1852. Nov. 30.—919. J. Barlow.
Stands or supports for casks, barrels, and other like vessels.

1853. Feb. 17.—415. M. Walker.
Vessels or apparatus for containing and preserving ale, beer, and other liquids.

„ Mar. 3.—543. J. Waterman.
Treating brewery and distillery grains for the production of food for cattle, and for extracting the bitter principle and other products from the refuse hops of breweries.

„ Oct. 8.—2304. H. Krant.
Stands for casks and barrels.

„ Dec. 22.—2973. J. Youill.
Method of obtaining power to raise liquids, treating the same liquids when raised, and using them to obtain additional power.

1854. Jan. 28.—209. J. J. L. Fournier.
Mode of obtaining alcohol.

1855. April 20.—882. J. A. Manning.
Effecting the agitation of fluids and solid matters contained therein.

1856. Jan. 15.—110. T. H. Bakewell.
Ventilating, warming, and cooling rooms and other places.

„ Feb. 14.—387. T. E. Blackwell.
Condensing steam, cooling, and heating fluids.

„ April 22.—966. T. E. Blackwell.
Treating water for the use of brewers.

1857. May 23.—1456. E. Travis and J. L. Casartelli.
An improved apparatus for regulating the supply and discharge of steam, air, water, and other fluids.

1858. April 10.—A. Manbré.
Manufacture of a colouring matter for colouring spirits, beverages, and other liquids, from the sugar of potatoes, known as glucose, and syrup de fecule.

„ July 14.—1583. F. Chapusot and V. Avril.
Producing a more or less perfect vacuum, and applying the same to industrial purposes.

1859. Feb. 24.—505. J. H. G. D. Wagner.
Apparatus for cleaning water and removing all matters in suspension.

„ Mar. 31.—803. C. Pickering.
Improved apparatus for brewing.

„ April 13.—923. J. Hill.
Wire screens.

„ May 11.—1178. A. Manbré.
An improved method of extracting and purifying sugar, called glucose and syrup de fecule, from potatoes, or fecula, or starch, or dextrine, for the purposes and uses of brewers, distillers, &c.

„ June 7.—1407. W. Clark.
Preservation of animal and vegetable matters.

„ Sept. 20.—2137. A Manbré.
Manufacture of a colouring matter for colouring spirits, beer, vinegar, and other liquids and beverages.

„ „ 20.—2138. A. Manbré.
An improved method of extracting and purifying sugar, called glucose and syrup de fecule, from potatoes, or fecula, or starch, or dextrine.

1860. Oct. 11.—2479. E. J. Harron.
Manufacture of vegetable albumine (for clarifying malt liquors).

1861. Feb. 13.—365. C. S. Roskilly.
Refining malt liquors.

„ Mar. 30.—792. H. Medlock.
Improved means of preserving fermented liquors.

„ June 13.—1520. J. Illingworth.
Improvements in arranging sizing houses, brewhouses, &c., to facilitate the removal of steam set free therein.

„ Aug. 30.—2158. S. Pluchart.
An improved beverage called "Moka" beer.

„ Nov. 19.—2901. L. and M. Smith.
Improvements in raising liquids, and in apparatus connected therewith, parts of which are applicable to improving the quality of fermented liquors.

„ Dec. 7.—3069. R. Jolly.
An improved apparatus for heating, cooling, or drying, infusing, extracting, or absorbing vapours or gases for manufacturing purposes, and for preserving liquids.

1862. Mar. 31.—887. M. A. F. Mennons.
Manufacture from vegetable product of glucose or fermentable sugar.

„ May 5.—1338. P. L. A. T. Sourbe.
An improved method of maturing spirits and wines.

„ „ 9.—1396. T. Welton.
Preparation of beverages in connection with brewing.

„ June 5.—1692. G. Rydill.
An improved hydraulic pump or engine for raising liquids and obtaining motive power, also applicable for the ventilation of wines, and other useful purposes.

„ „ 9.—1716. A. Ford.
An improved method of protecting beer and other fluids from the direct action of atmospheric air.

„ Dec. 18.—3396. J. L. W. Thudichum.
Improvements in the preservation of beer and other fermented liquids, and in the apparatus and means to be employed therein.

1863. Feb. 3.—304. J. Fletcher and H. Bower.
An improved injector or apparatus for feeding boilers with water (or pump for breweries).

„ April 1.—839. W. Clark.
Improvements in preventing fermentation in alcoholic and other liquids while drawing them from their containing vessels, and in apparatus for the same.

„ „ 1.—844. R. Gavin.
Preservation of perishable liquids during the withdrawal or consumption thereof.

„ June 26.—1609. W. Clark.
Apparatus for aerating liquids.

„ July 6.—1677. S. J. Cooke.
Improvements in apparatus for supplying carbonic acid gas to cask or other vessels containing beer or other fermented liquid.

„ „ 16.—1780. S. A. Cooper.
An improved packing-case to contain bottled beer.

1864. Feb. 6.—322. W. R. Taylor.
Brewing utensils.

„ Mar. 4.—551. S. Bourne.
Casks and other vessels for containing beer and other liquids that are injured when exposed to atmospheric air.

„ „ 4.—552. A. Manbré.
Manufacture of glucose sugar.

„ Nov. 12.—2821. F. A. Papps.
Improvements in malt liquors as tonics.

1865. Mar. 22.—799. W. J. Coleman.
An improved composition for clarifying and fining beer and other fermented liquors.

„ Nov. 10.—2898. E. J. Davis.
Treating brewers' grains, in order to render them more suitable for the food of animals.

„ Dec. 12.—3203. J. Kaspary.
A new and improved compound, to be employed as a drinking beverage.

1866. Jan. 4.—34. F. Wright.
A new preparation of fruit beverages of a stimulating character.

„ Feb. 23.—565. R. Millburn, jun., and W. H. Baxter.
Treatment of brewers' and distillers' grains.

„ April 3.—949. A. G. Lock.
Preparation and application of malt grains or brewers' refuse as a manure.

„ „ 5.—985. W. R. Taylor and G. Hewett.
Improvements in the treatment of grain and raw spirit, and in the apparatus employed therein.

„ May 9.—1326. J. H. Johnson.
Improvements in machinery or apparatus for drying and cooling grain, applicable also to the manufacture of malt.

„ „ 23.—1445. E. Gripper.
Treatment of grains from brewers, distillers, &c.; rendering them more suitable for the food of cattle, and as a substitute for patent malt.

„ Oct. 30.—J. Varley.
Apparatus for supplying or feeding water to steam boilers (measuring wort).

„ Dec. 29.—3422. J. Slatter.
An improved screen or sifter for screening cinders, corn, tea, sugar, gravel, malt, &c.

1867. Jan. 18.—130. D. W. Hamper.
Preparation of finings for fining or clearing fermented liquors.

„ Feb. 9.—379. W. Clark.
Preserving animal or vegetable matters, whether fluid or solid, in a wholesome and edible condition, without material loss or change of their natural flavour.

„ May 1.—1267. J. L. Norton.
Drying machines.

„ „ 2.—1289. C. Ritchie.
Apparatus for storing and drawing off beer, wine, and other materials.

„ „ 9.—1380. C. Ritchie.
Improvements in casks, and in apparatus for storing and drawing off liquids and semi-fluid matters.

„ „ 13.—1421. W. Sodo.
An improved method of, and apparatus for, drawing off and refining liquors, or liquids of any kind.

„ „ 14.—1427. A. M. Clark.
Improvements in the means of raising liquids, and in apparatus for the same.

„ June 10.—1698. J. Crompton.
Apparatus for, and modes of, revivifying malt liquors and other beverages, and for warming them.

„ „ 13.—1729. T. S. Prideaux.
Improving wine on draught, and of apparatus to be used for this object, also applicable to other liquids.

„ July 13.—2071. J. L. Norton.
Apparatus for drying grain, seed, malt, spent hops, brewers' and distillers' grains, &c.

„ „ 15.—2081. J. Fleming.
Apparatus for drawing or raising beer, and other malt or spirituous liquors to a higher level than that of the cask or vessel in which they are kept.

„ „ 20.—2122. T. Broomwich.
An improved means of allowing the escape of superfluous carbon from casks of newly made wine, cider, perry, and other fermenting liquors.

„ Nov. 16.—3260. J. G. Tongue.
Process and apparatus employed for ageing and refining wines, spirits, and other liquors.

„ Dec. 9.—3499. L. Rose.
An improved mode of preserving vegetable juices.

„ „ 14.—3566. A. M. Clark.
Improvements in the extraction of ammonia from fermented and other liquids, and in the regeneration of the agents used in such extraction.

1868. Jan. 9.—86. C. H. Newman.
Manufacture of unfermented and unintoxicating malt liquors.

„ „ 17.—171. J. Winter, jun.
Improved apparatus for filling bottles, also machinery in combination with the above apparatus, for corking or stoppering such said bottles.

„ „ 22.—228. S. Bennett.
Means or apparatus to facilitate the drying of grain, seed, brewers' grains, and other matters.

„ Feb. 3.—360. J. and W. Weems.
Machinery, apparatus, or means for heating and drying grain, and other vegetable products.

1868. Mar. 17.—898. R. Smith.
Means and apparatus for extracting foul air and gases from mines, sewers, brewers' vats, and other places.

„ „ 27.—1048. A. Scott.
The production of an alcoholic fermented drink, of which tea or coffee is an essential ingredient.

„ May 11.—1535. A. M. Dix.
An improved mode of, and apparatus for, supplying finings or other liquids to casks or other vessels.

„ „ 28.—1760. W. E. Newton.
Improved apparatus for hopping beer.

„ July 20.—2278. L. Rose.
An improved aerated liquid, or artificial champagne.

„ Aug. 15.—2558. W. B. Espeut.
Improvements in curing, drying, and extracting molasses or liquid from sugar and other substances, and in apparatus employed therein.

„ „ 17.—2561. E. Beanes.
Manufacture of brewers' finings.

„ „ 31.—2695. L. F. A. P. Riviere.
Cases for packing bottles containing wine or other liquid.

„ Sept. 14.—2820. F. Seebohe-Ultzen.
Improved apparatus for generating carbonic acid, applicable to beer casks and other vessels, for preserving, raising, and transferring their contents.

„ Oct. 29.—3314. H. Wallwork.
Taps or valves.

1869. Jan. 1.—F. Perry.
An improved process for preserving animal and vegetable substances, and also for preserving fermented liquors.

„ Feb. 8.—381. L. S. A. Seckbach.
Improvements in the method of, and apparatus for, preserving, improving, and discharging beer.

„ Mar. 20.—847. J. Hamilton and R. Paterson.
Improvements in apparatus for containing, treating, preserving, cooling, and conveying fermentable beverages.

„ April 4.—1370. W. E. Gedge.
An auto-dynamic carbonic acid gas apparatus for raising liquids, &c.

„ June 14.—1818. J. Taylor.
A floating or sliding top for wells, tanks, cisterns, &c.

„ Aug. 24.—2519. J. Valters.
An improved agent for fining and clarifying ale, &c.

„ Nov. 18.—3327. M. Shelley.
An improved vent peg.

„ Dec. 18.—3661. J. C. Martin.
An improvement in the manufacture of finings.

„ „ „ —3671. S. Giles.
Improvement in apparatus to be used in the fermentation of worts.

1870. Jan. 26.—241. W. J. Coleman.
Treating sour beer to remove its acidity.

„ Feb. 18.—481. R. Hunt.
An improved apparatus or receptacle for storing and withdrawing wine or other liquid.

„ Mar. 31.—137. A. B. Reis.
A new or improved apparatus, applicable to barrels, &c., for the preservation of fermented liquors.

1870. April 7.—1029. C. Clinch.
Apparatus for cleansing beer.
„ „ 12.—1062. C. H. Newman.
An improved invention for producing an unintoxicating malt liquor.
„ July 18.—2021. Sir G. A. Terry.
Apparatus for preparing finings.
„ Aug. 3.—2167. W. R. Lake.
An improved method of, and apparatus for, refining liquors.
„ „ 12.—2245. J. Gale and H. Ormston.
An improved machine for reducing isinglass or brewers' finings.
„ Sept. 8.—2429. W. Silcock.
An improved screen wire.
„ „ 20.—2822. A. Frankenburg.
Apparatus for raising, drawing off, and cooling liquids.
„ Oct. 1.—2618. F. J. Head.
Construction of cocks and valves.
„ „ 17.—2732. M. Smith, G. F. Waldener, and A. C. Lee.
Raising and registering the measurement of wine, &c.
„ Nov. 11.—2969. E. Herring.
Manufacture of alkalized isinglass.
„ „ 24.—3076. W. T. Read.
Purifying beer.
„ Dec. 13.—3264. A. W. Gillman and Spencer.
Treatment of beer, ale, &c.
1871. Mar. 7.—607. A. W. Gillman and Spencer.
Improvements in the treatment of beer.
„ April 20.—1044. B. J. B. Mills.
Improvements in method and apparatus in the manufacture of beer.
„ Aug. 2.—2040. W. J. Curtis.
Improved means and apparatus for obtaining extracts and filtering liquids.
„ Nov. 27.—3200. E. Gregory.
A new or improved instrument to be used in fining.
1872. Jan. 31.—314. W. A. Gibbs and A. Borwick.
Improvements in apparatus for drying.
„ Feb. 1.—327. W. J. Curtis.
Improved means of, and apparatus for, obtaining extracts.
„ June 10.—1750. C. J. Smith.
An improved coupling for hose.
„ Oct. 18.—3078. J. Hamilton and R. Paterson.
Improvements in aerating or racking.
„ „ „ —3080. H. Bethell.
Improvements in the treatment of beers.
1873. Feb. 18.—599. C. W. Sutton.
Improved combinations for removing acidity from ales.
„ „ 22.—682. A. M. Clark.
Improvements in the purification of sugar.
„ July 14.—2421. W. H. Baxter.
Improvements in self-acting, weighing, and measuring machines.
„ „ 17.—2470. E. G. Wright.
Improved apparatus for cutting brewers' finings.
„ Sept. 17.—3056. A. W. Gillman and S. Spencer.
Improvements in the manufacture of beer.
„ Nov. 27.—3877. A. Tooth.
Improvements in the treatment of beer.
„ Dec. 5.—4001. T. G. Messenger.
Improvements in pipe-joints.

1874. Jan. 1.—16. L. Deny.
An improved mode of forming strainers.
„ „ 23.—289. P. E. Lockwood.
An improved method of treating beer.
„ April 20.—1361. R. E. Southby.
Improvements for destroying acidity in beer.
„ May 8.—1626. D. Nicholl.
Improvements in vessels containing aerated and other liquids.
„ „ 13.—1705. A. M. Clark.
An improvement in the manufacture of beer (concentrated beer).
„ Dec. 4.—4180. W. Bruce.
An improved method for fining ale.
1875. Jan. 20.—213. G. Shand.
Improvements in treating malt liquor.
„ „ 21.—234. A. W. Gillman and S. Spencer.
An improved method of treating beer.
„ July 22.—2609. F. Dixon.
Improvements in the treatment of wood casks.
„ „ 31.—2712. C. B. Gibbond and R. Allison.
Improved means of preserving beers.
„ Oct. 23.—3687. F. N. G. Gill.
Improvements in manufacture of beer (charging wort with alcohol).
„ Dec. 21.—4418. H. B. Barlow.
Improvement in the construction of filters.
1876. Mar. 2.—901. G. H. Gill.
Manufacture of beer.
1877. Feb. 5.—486. Drake.
Compound for enamelling brewing pans.
„ Sept. 1.—3332. Burbidge.
Using soluble salts of salicylic acid for preserving.
„ Nov. 5.—4106. Searle.
Syphon ventilator for breweries.
„ Dec. 1.—4547. Searle.
Steam extractor for malt, &c., kilns.
1878. Nov. 28.—4842. Isitt.
Cleansing compound for brewers' utensils.
1879. Jan. 25.—320. Holland.
Ale or beer finings.
„ July 31.—3107. Gillman and Spence.
Brewers' casks.

LONDON: PRINTED BY WM. CLOWES AND SONS, LIMITED, STAMFORD STREET AND CHARING CROSS.

5 QUARTER BREWERY.

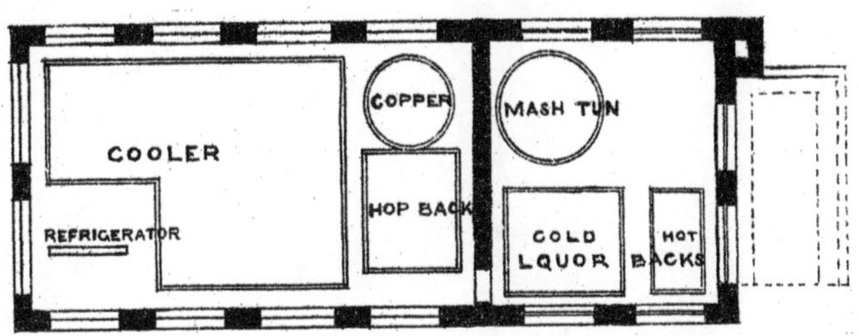

PLAN

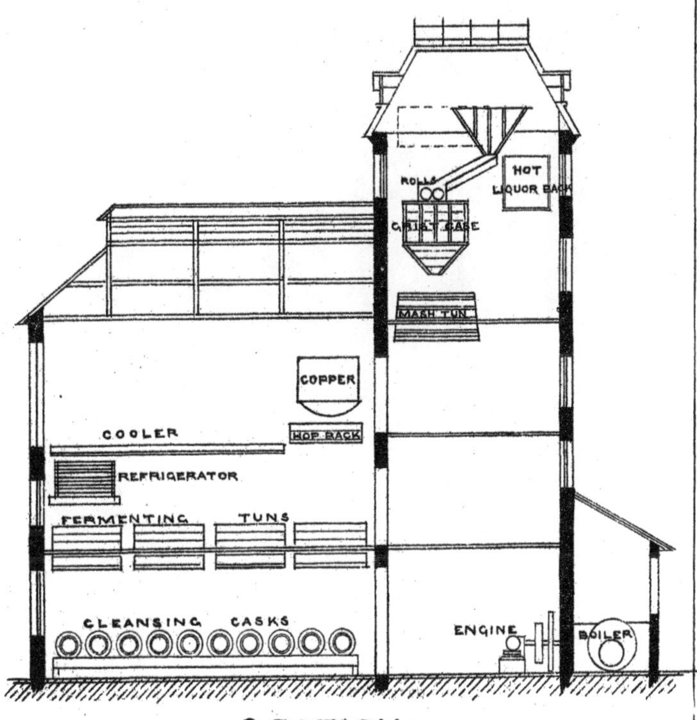

SECTION

Thomas Kell & Son, Photolith.

7 QUARTER BREWERY.

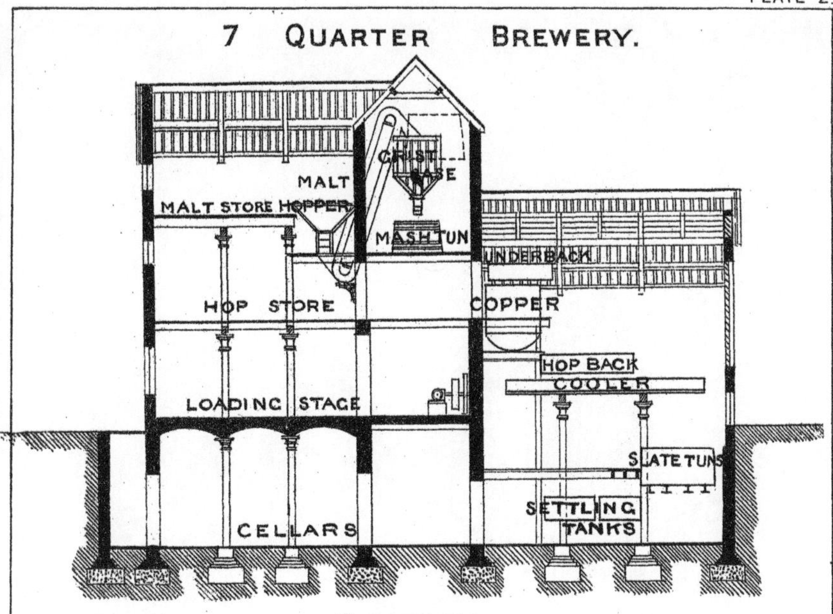

SECTION

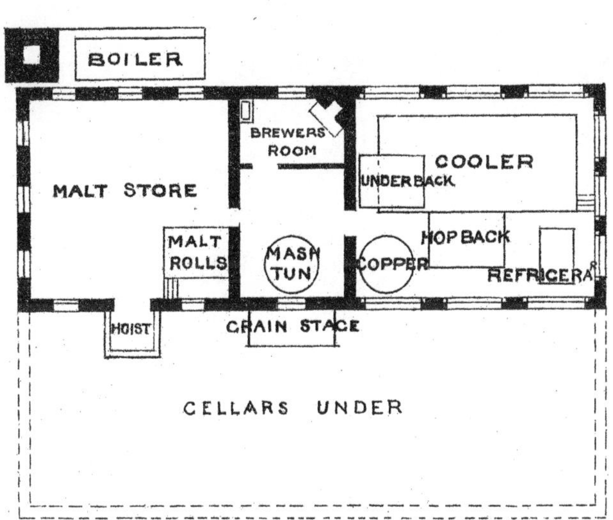

PLAN

SCALE OF 10 5 0 10 20 30 40 50 FEET

Thomas Kell & Son, Photolith.

10 QUARTER BREWERY.

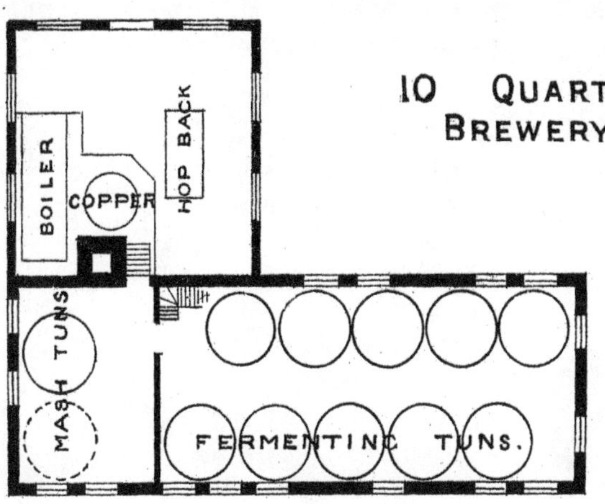

PLAN

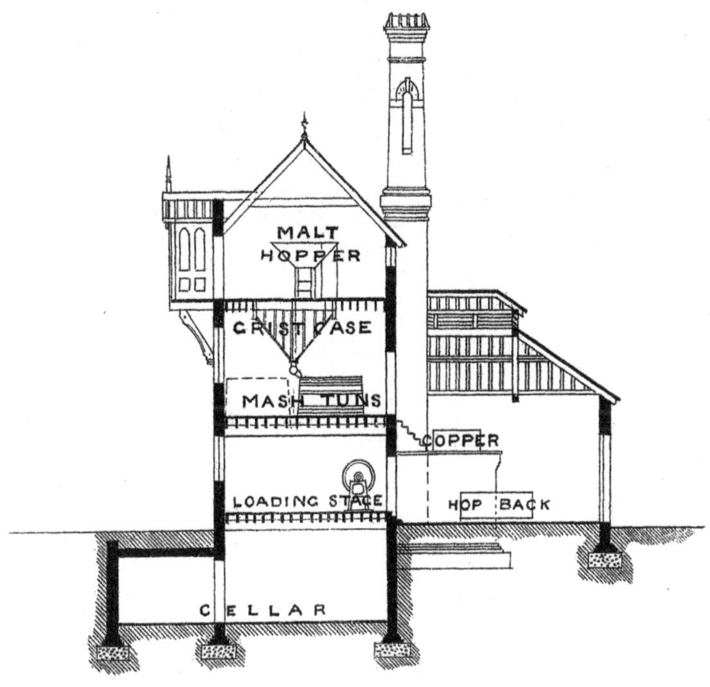

SECTION

SCALE OF 10 5 0 10 20 30 40 50 FEET

Thomas Kell & Son, Photolith.

15 QUARTER BREWERY.

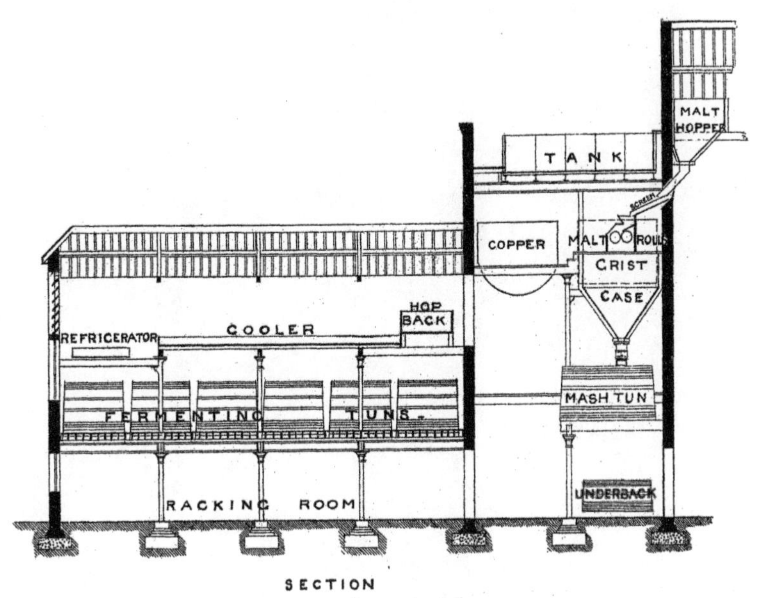

SECTION

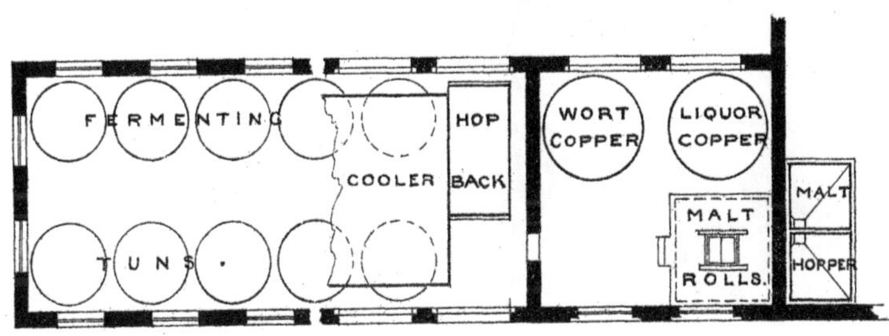

PLAN.

SCALE OF 10 5 0 10 20 30 40 50 FEET.

Thomas Kell & Son, Photolith.

16 QUARTER BREWERY.

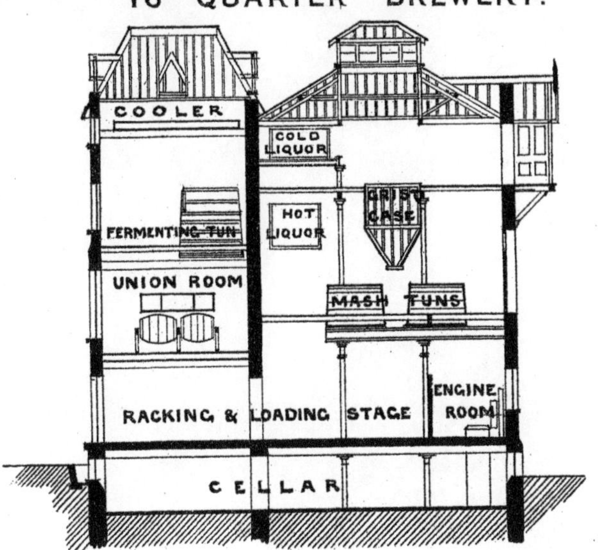

SECTION

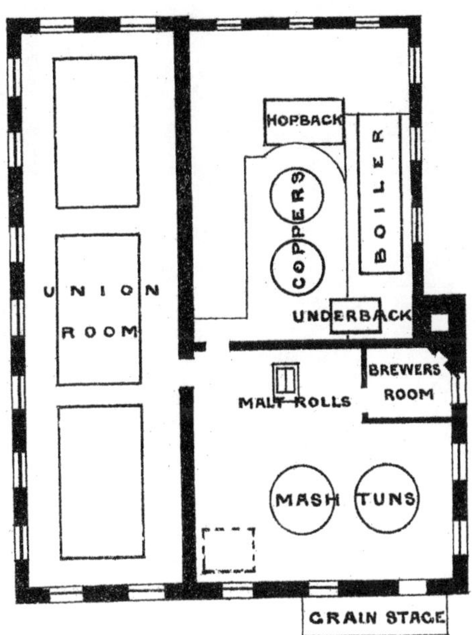

PLAN.

SCALE OF 10 5 0 10 20 30 40 50 FEET.

Thomas Kell & Son, Photolith.

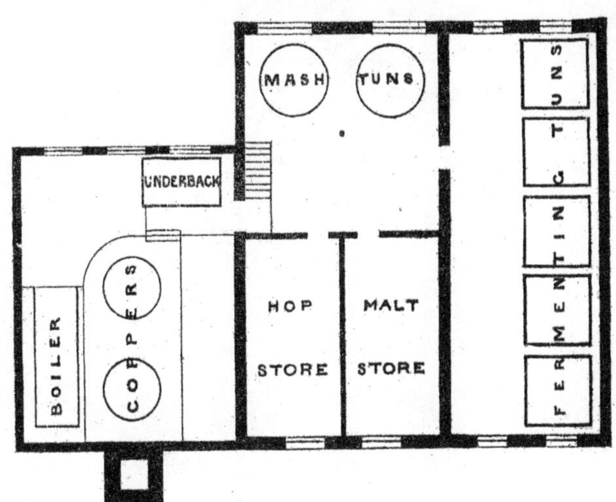

PLAN

20 QUARTER BREWERY.

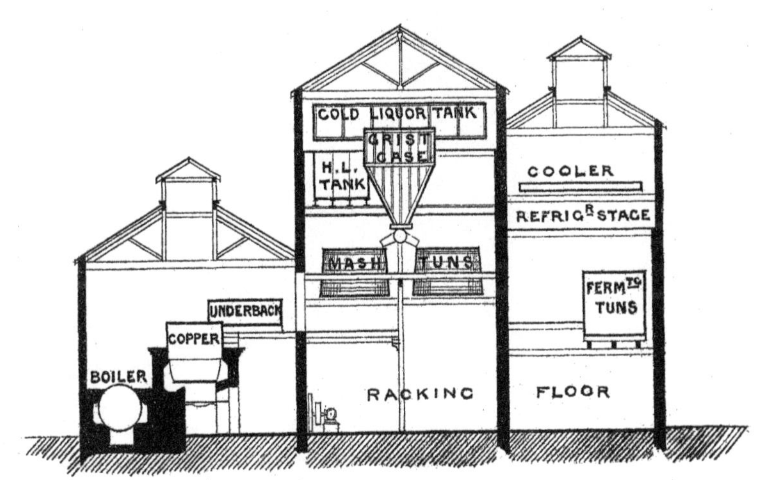

SECTION.

SCALE OF 10 5 0 10 20 30 40 50 FEET

Thomas Kell & Son, Photolith.

24 QUARTER BREWERY.

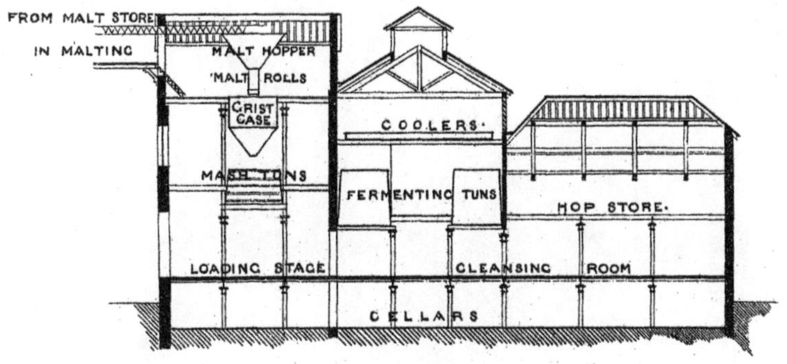

SECTION

CHY. SHAFT
BOILER
COPPERS
HOP BACK
REFRIGERATOR
BREWERS Rᴹ
MASH TUN STAGE
MASH
TUNS.
TUN ROOM
HOP STORE

PLAN

SCALE 0 5 10 10 20 30 40 50 OF FEET

Thomas Kell & Son, Photolith.

40 QUARTER BREWERY.

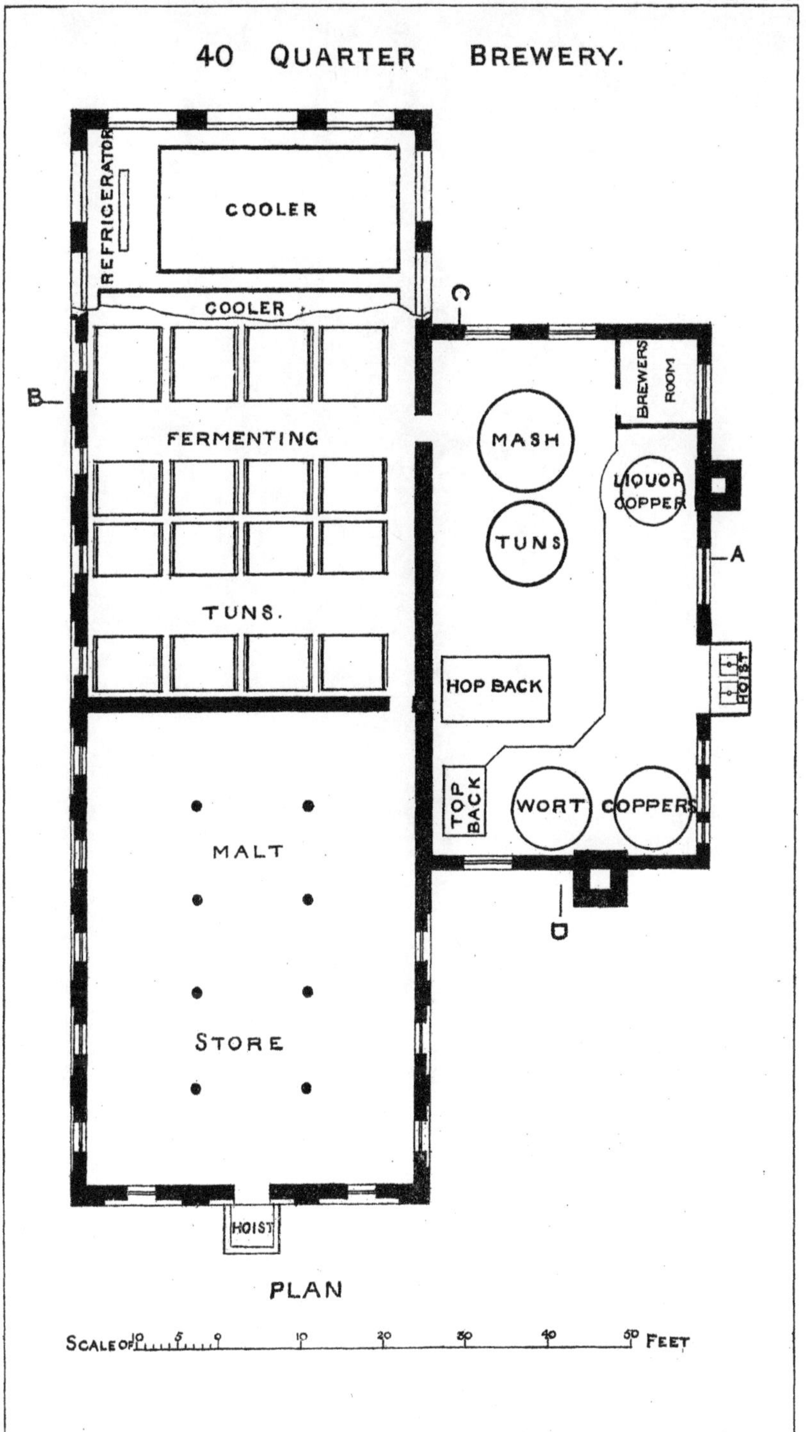

PLAN

Thomas Kell & Son, Photolith.

40 QUARTER BREWERY.

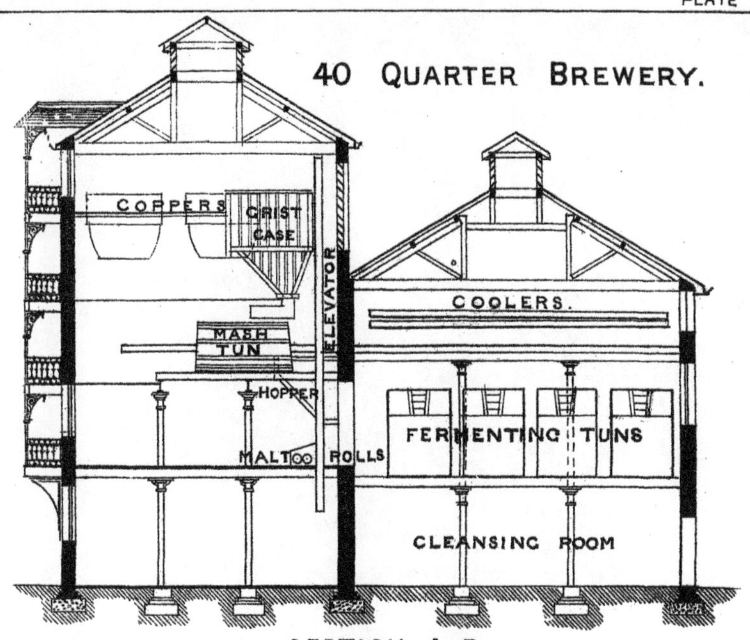

SECTION A.B.

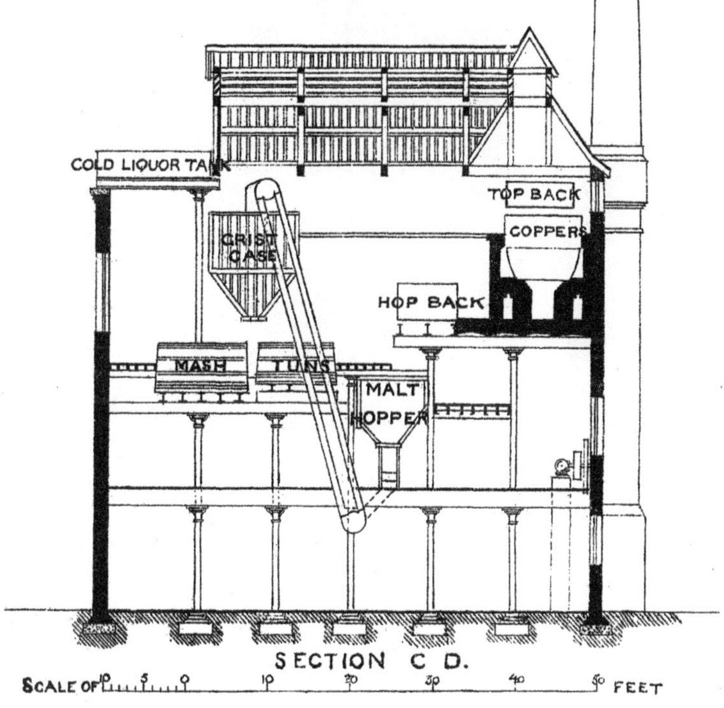

SECTION C D.

SCALE OF 10 5 0 10 20 30 40 50 FEET

Thomas Kell & Son, Photolith.

PLATE 10.

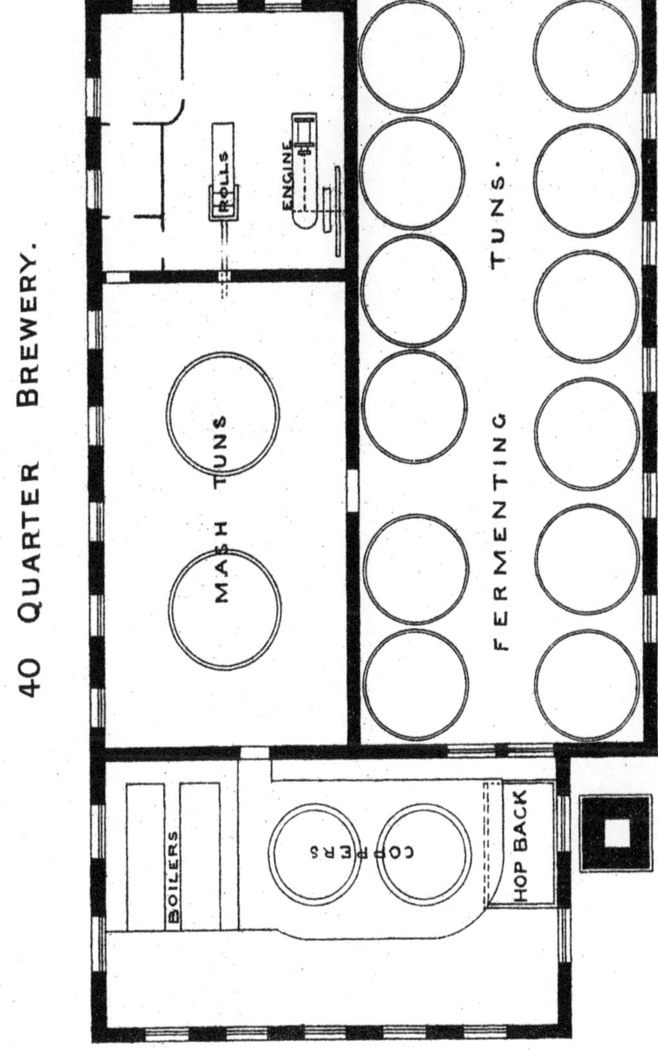

PLAN OF MASH TUN STAGE &c.

10 5 0 10 20 30 40 FEET.

Thomas Kell & Son, Photolith.

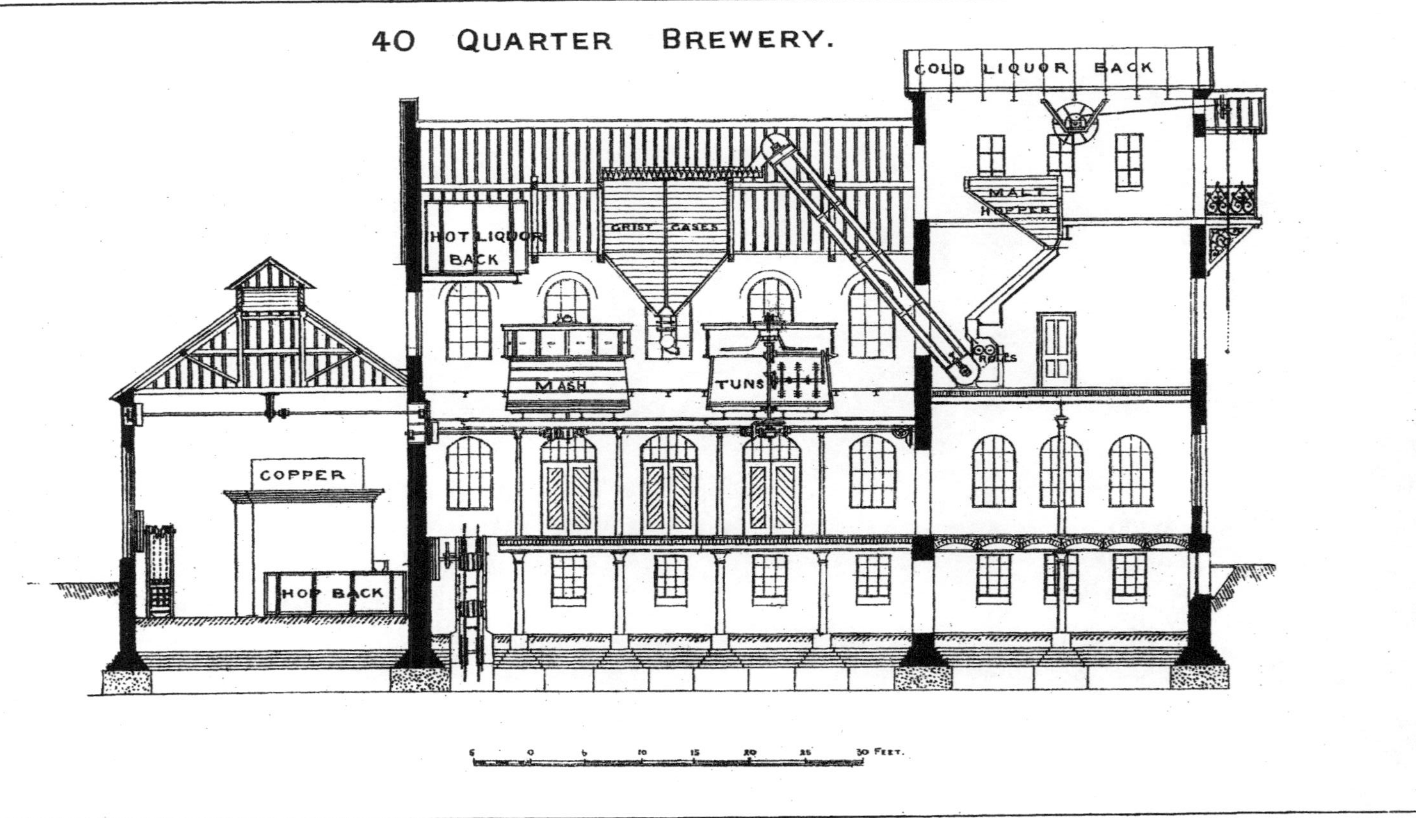

Thomas Kell & Son. Photolith.

PLATE 12.

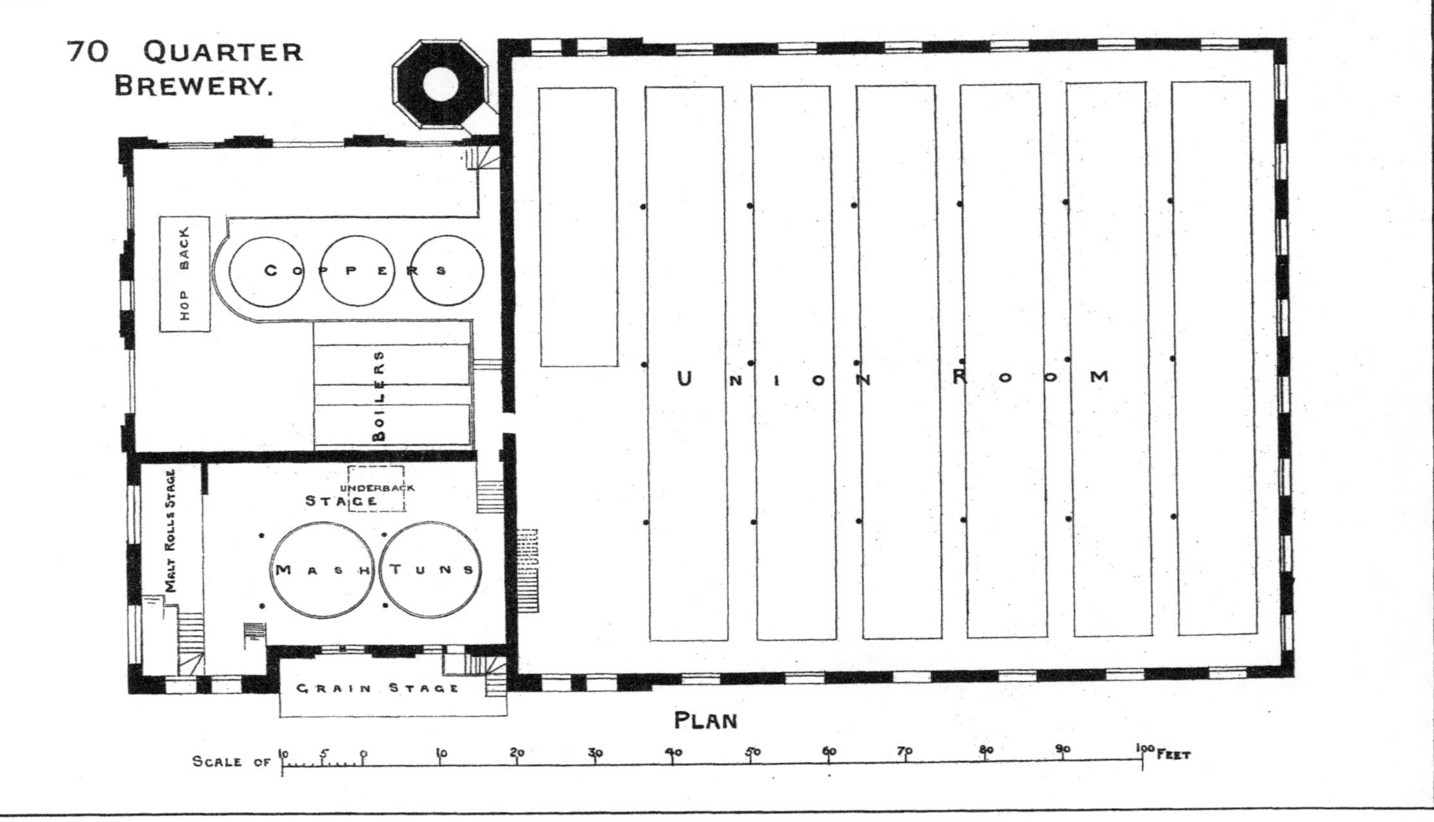

Thomas Kell & Son, Photolith.

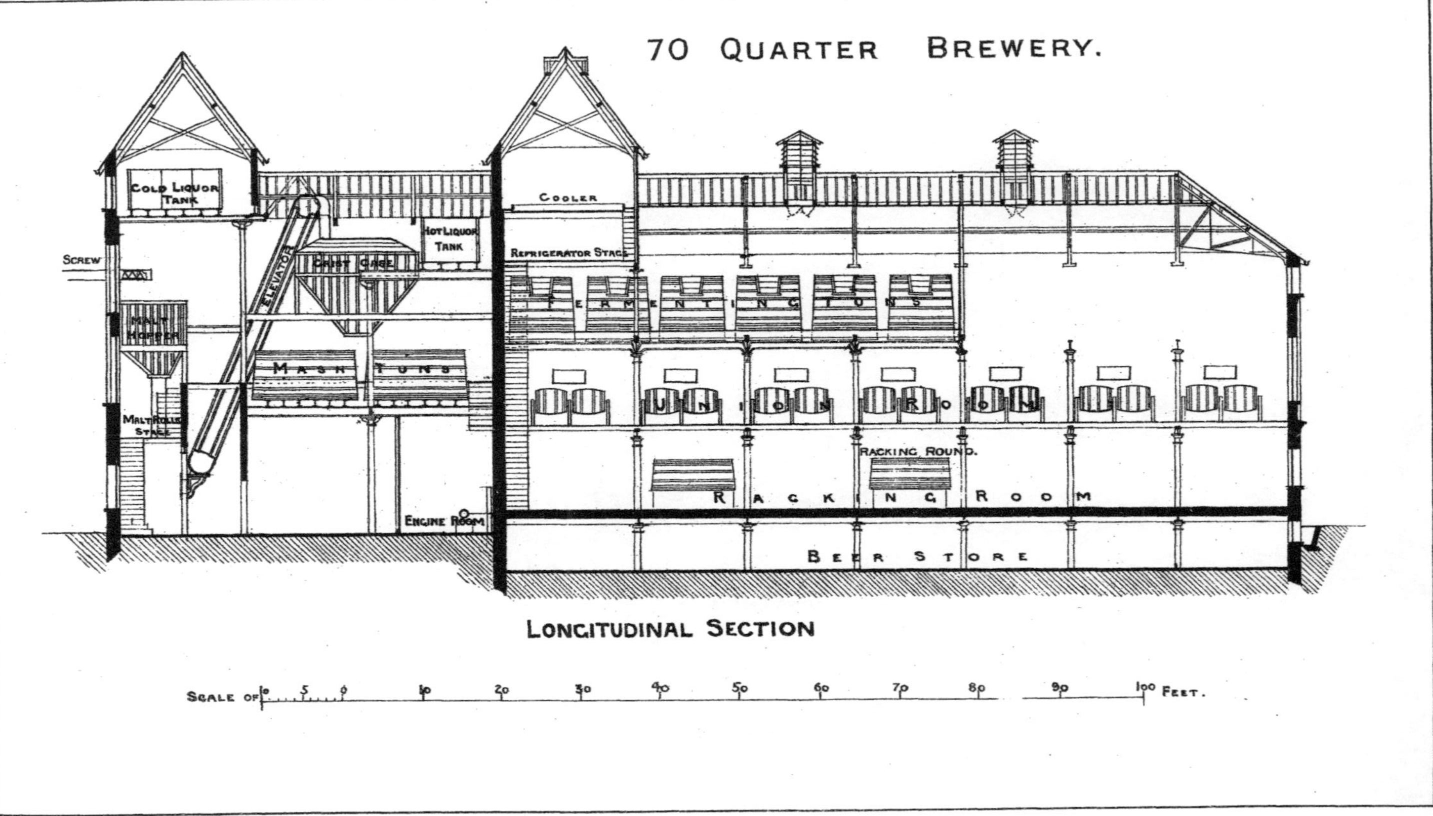

LONGITUDINAL SECTION

Thomas Kell & Son, Photolith.

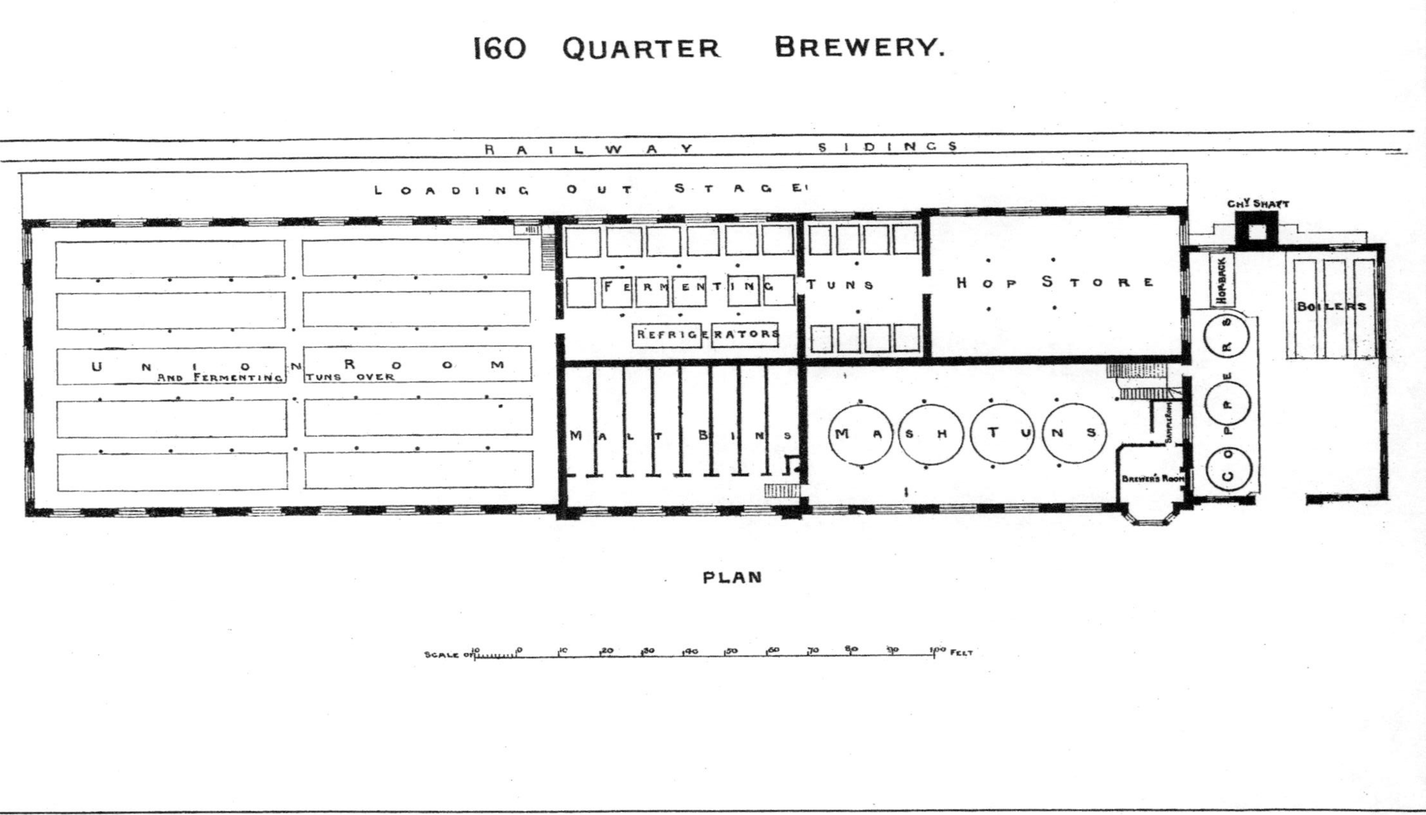

Thomas Kell & Son, Photolith.

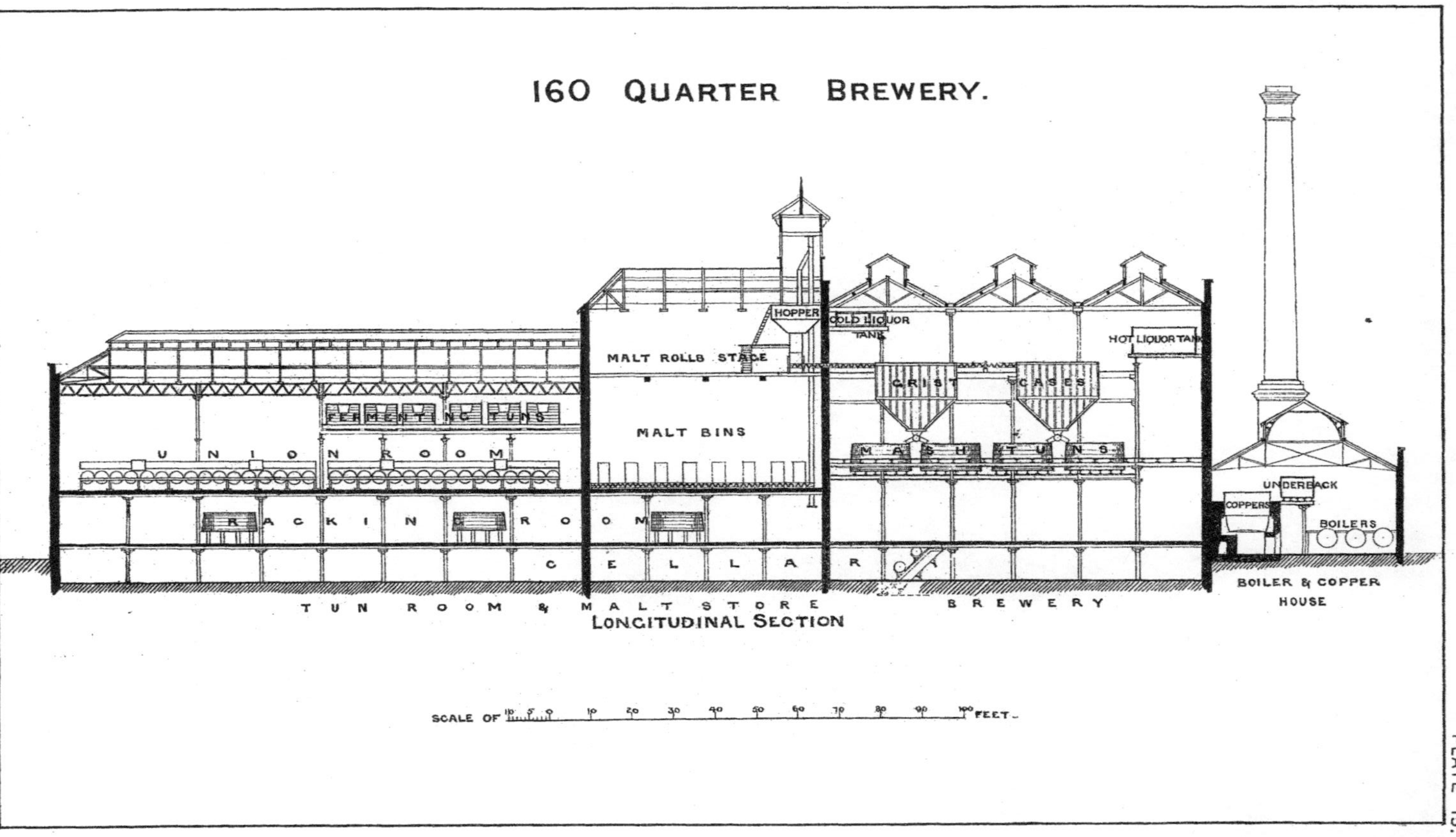

Thomas Kell & Son, Photolith.

PLATE 16.

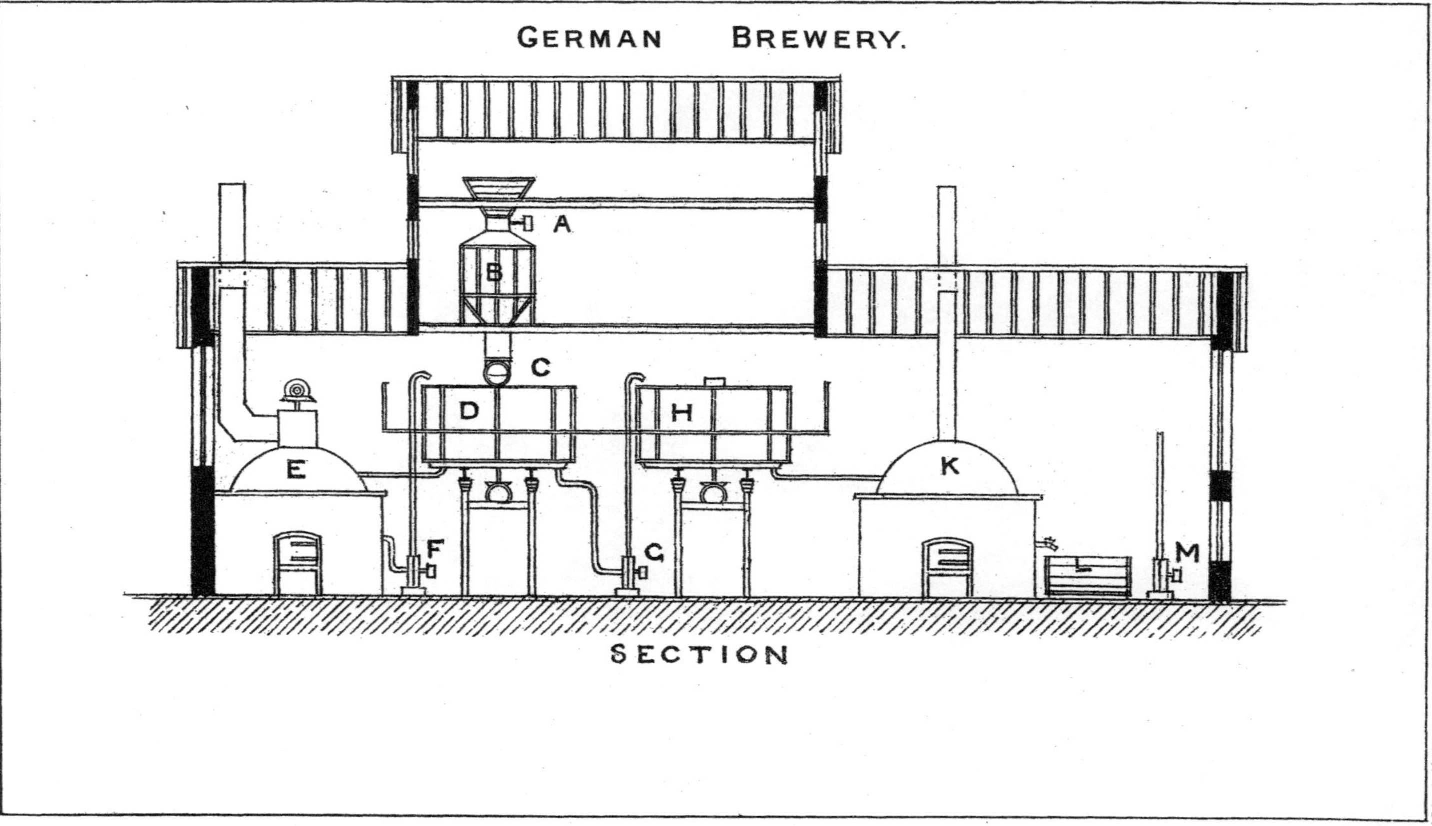

Thomas Kell & Son, Photolith.

GERMAN BREWERY.

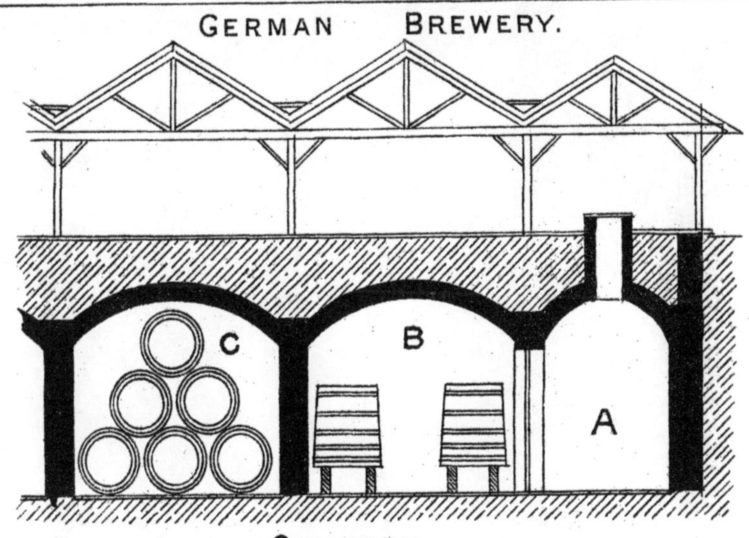

SECTION

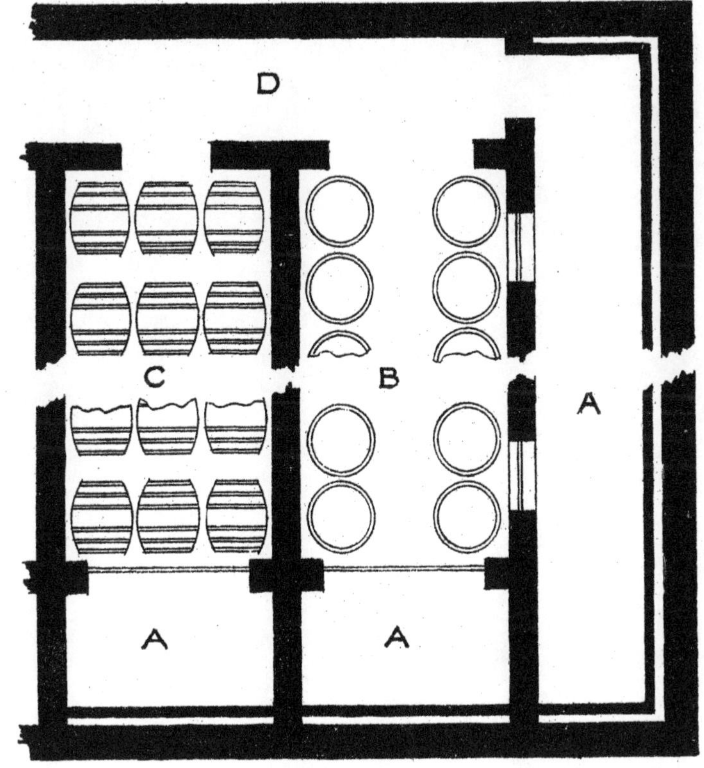

PLAN

Thomas Kell & Son, Photolith.

PLATE 18.

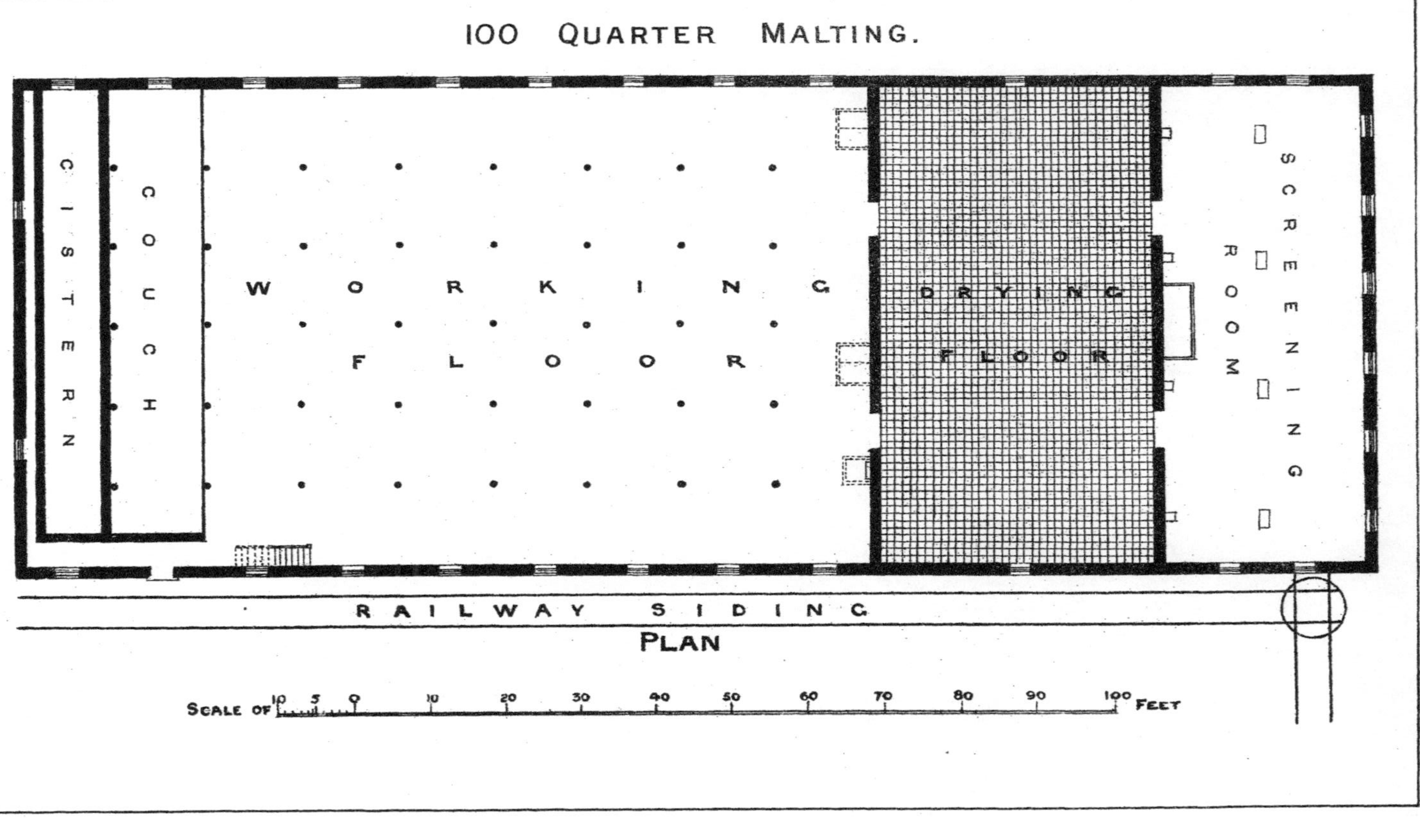

Thomas Kell & Son, Photolith.

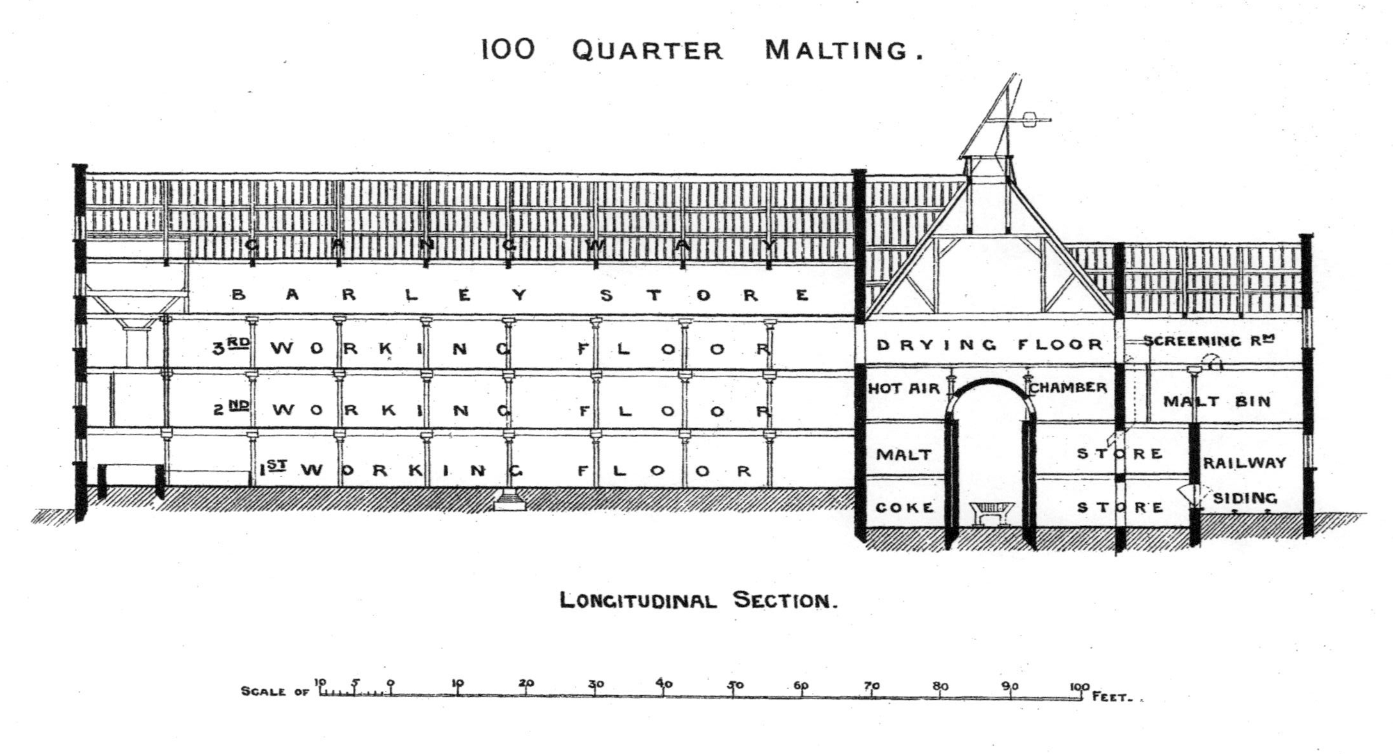

Thomas Kell & Son, Photolith.

GERMAN MALTING.

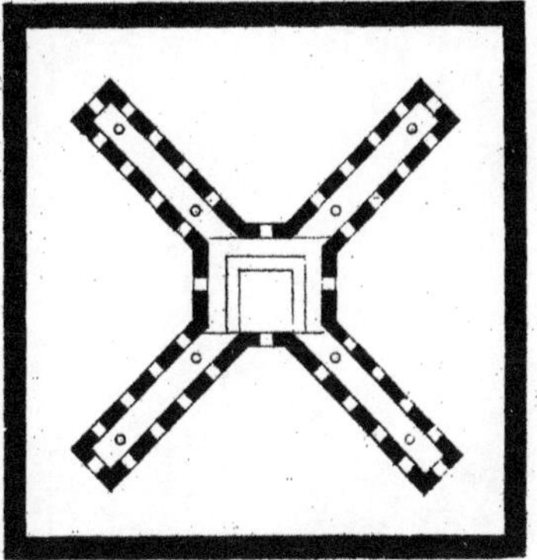

PLAN OF HOT AIR CHAMBER

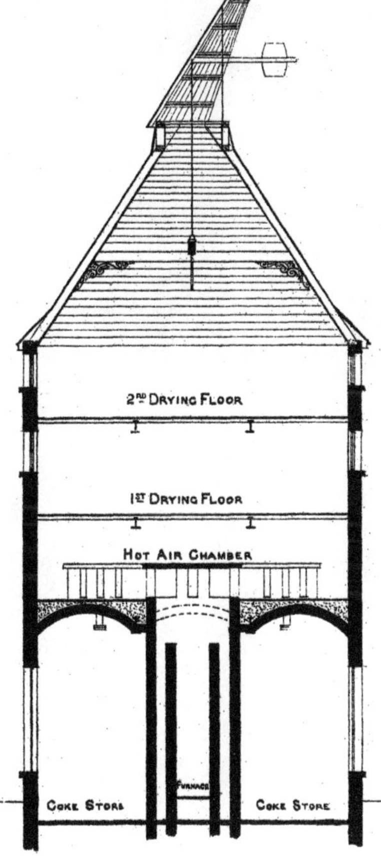

SECTION A.B

SCALE

0 5 10 20 30 FEET

Thomas Kell & Son, Photolith.

www.ingramcontent.com/pod-product-compliance
Lightning Source LLC
Chambersburg PA
CBHW030754150426
42813CB00068B/3065/J

* 9 7 8 0 9 8 3 6 3 8 9 9 5 *